The CUSTOM FURNITURE SOURCE BOOK

The *CUSTOM* FURNITURE SOURCE BOOK

A Guide to 125 Craftsmen

KERRY PIERCE

The Taunton Press

The Taunton Press
Inspiration for hands-on living™

The Taunton Press, Inc., 63 South Main Street, PO Box 5506, Newtown, CT 06470-5506
e-mail: tp@taunton.com

Distributed by Publishers Group West

COVER DESIGN AND LAYOUT: Ann Marie Manca
INTERIOR DESIGN: Lynne Phillips
INTERIOR LAYOUT: Carol Petro

LIBRARY OF CONGRESS CATALOGING-IN-PUBLICATION DATA:
Pierce, Kerry.
   The custom furniture sourcebook : a guide to 125 craftsmen / Kerry Pierce.
     p. cm.
  ISBN 1-56158-431-2
   1. Furniture making--United States--Directories. 2. Cabinetmakers--United
States--Directories. I. Title.

TT194 .P52 2001
749'.025'73--dc21   2001035156

Acknowledgments

I'D LIKE TO THANK Marc Adams, Jon Binzen, and Art Carpenter, who labored through two long days last summer to jury the work submitted for this book. Their broad and deep knowledge of contemporary woodworking lent credibility to the otherwise subjective process of evaluating the work of contemporary furniture makers.

I would also like to thank everybody at The Taunton Press who together supplied me with an extraordinary level of support. In particular, I'd like to thank my editor Jennifer Renjilian for her good sense and mature judgment; Helen Albert, the executive editor, whose enthusiasm for this title matched my own; and Meredith DeSousa, who managed to bring order to the complex process of jurying the many portfolios we were given to review.

And of course, I'd like to thank the men and women who agreed to share their work on the pages of this book. Without that work and their willingness to share that work, there would be no book.

And Elaine, Emily, and Andy. Always.

Contents

Introduction

IN THE WORLD OF FURNITURE, sometimes "good" isn't good enough. Whether you're buying for yourself or for a client, sometimes you need something really special, something at the very top of the quality ladder. You can't find that work in a furniture store or a manufacturer's catalog. You have to go to the source, to the men and women whose refined sensibility and meticulous craftsmanship enable them to produce truly distinctive furniture. Bringing you to the source, to those craftsmen, is what this book is all about.

Here on these pages you will see the work of some of North America's finest furniture makers. Their portfolios were juried by a panel of experts: one a renowned independent furniture maker for almost a half century, another the director of one of the largest woodworking schools in the United States, and the third a former editor of *Home Furniture* and *Fine Woodworking* magazines.

Choice is one of the most important benefits of working directly with the men and women who create the furniture you intend to purchase. In addition to their signature pieces, many of the makers represented on these pages also do custom work. This permits you, the buyer, to have a voice in the finished work.

This book provides you with all the information you'll need to contact the craftsmen whose work appears on these pages. You'll also find a regional index to help you locate makers in your area and a style index to help you quickly identify those individuals working in your favorite styles and periods. In the beginning of the book, you'll find lots of tips to guide you through the process of buying the kind of work you see represented here.

The purchase of fine furniture can be an exhilarating experience. Enjoy the process.

Purchasing Custom Furniture

IS THE PURCHASE of good custom furniture worth the effort? The short answer to the question is yes. Good, custom furniture makes sense to your wallet because it appreciates over time, unlike factory-built furniture, which is likely to depreciate from the moment it's loaded onto a truck for delivery to your home.

The long answer to the question is also yes. Good custom furniture is worth the effort it may require because it can enrich your life in ways that can't be approximated by factory-built furniture. Good custom furniture provides you with enduring visual and tactile pleasure, in addition to a functionality precisely attuned to your specific needs. It's furniture that wears well and will bring as much pleasure into your life 20 years from now as it does today. It is, in fact, furniture that will become a part of the legacy you will leave to your family.

The process does take some effort. Custom furniture can't be purchased on impulse. It must be sought out. But the effort isn't distasteful. In fact, that effort, the exploration of your own needs and tastes, the investigation of furniture styles and materials, and the interaction with the maker all can add meaning to the experience of furnishing your home.

> *"Enjoy having exactly what you want made for your pleasure. Know that museum-quality furniture will last and have meaning and value for generations."*
>
> TIMOTHY S. PHILBRICK, NARRAGANSETT, R.I.

MAKER: Abbott Norris, Jon Roske

What Do You Want?

Just as the purchase of a new car should be preceded by a bit of research, so too should the purchase of custom furniture. But fortunately this research doesn't require hours in the library. Instead, it's primarily focused on your personal needs and expectations.

You should begin by articulating what it is you want your furniture to do. Is it intended to house a collection of art pottery? To provide your family with enough table space to sit a half-dozen guests? Or to hide your TV, VCR, and stereo receiver? If there are to be drawers, what will be stored in those drawers? If the piece is to be a cabinet with doors, how many doors do you need and how many shelves would you like inside those doors?

As you're clarifying the intended function, you should also be considering furniture styles. It isn't necessary to study books on period furniture or other furniture styles, although you may find it helpful to become familiar with the design terms associated with the style

MAKER:
Dave Sawyer

MAKER: Randy Weersing

you like to give you more confidence when communicating with the furniture maker.

Regardless of your book research, you should keep a record of pieces that have caught your eye. That record could consist of magazine clippings, photos, sketches, even verbal descriptions.

"Read about the furniture and wood. The more you know about style and species, the more rewarding your experience will be."

MARK ARNOLD, SUNBURY, OHIO

The Setting Determines the Size

You must also decide where the furniture will go. A restored 18th-century farmhouse might be an ideal setting for hand-built country-style reproduction furniture, but it might make a less comfortable setting for contemporary studio furniture. You should also consider the furniture that will be near the new piece. You may not want to place a chair with riven and shaved oak posts beside a high-style period secretary built of quilted mahogany.

Your consideration of site will also help you determine the dimensions of the finished piece. A towering 18th-century highboy with a flamboyant cartouche won't fit in a room with 7-ft. ceilings. And a petite display cabinet perched atop four delicate legs will appear lost as the only piece of furniture along a 25-ft. expanse of wall.

Your own personal dimensions can also impinge on the issue of dimensions. A man who stands 6'3" won't be very comfortable in a #5 Shaker chair reproduction. Similarly, a woman who stands 5'2" may not want a chest of drawers in which the top drawer opens several inches above her head.

Find a Craftsman

Once the issues of purpose, style, setting, and size have begun to take shape in your mind, it's time to talk to craftsmen. How do you find them? Well, you're holding in your hands one good resource, but there are others.

Shows devoted exclusively to furniture are often staged by woodworker associations, but even if there are no such associations in your area, a careful search will likely reveal some high-level craft shows at which three or four (or maybe a dozen) furniture makers display their work along with the work of potters, fiber artists, and others. Galleries, too, can put you in touch with the work of top-level makers and can provide a good setting for making first contact with the kind of work you wish to own. But high-level shows do something more: They put you face to face with the maker of that work.

Go to the shows. Visit the craftsmen. Talk to them. And of course, look at the work itself. Is the primary wood (the wood visible on the outside of the piece) of good quality? Is it authentic (mahogany, walnut, or

MAKER: Jeff Miller

cherry, rather than some other wood stained or dyed to look like one of these)? Has the maker paid attention to the wood's figure in the construction process? The grain doesn't have to all run in the same direction, but a top-level maker will arrange the figure so that it makes good visual sense, by, for example, book-matching joined sheets of veneer or choosing similarly figured material for all the back slats on an individual chair.

Run your hands over the surfaces. Any roughness (or inconsistently reflected light) is evidence of a finish that was not applied well.

Pull out the drawers. Do they work smoothly? Is the fit consistent along the entire length of the drawer's extension?

Talk to the craftsman about joinery. Is it cut by hand or by machine? Some good craftsmen will use machines to cut their joinery, but as you'll see from reading this book, many top-level craftsmen cut their joinery by hand.

And of course, look at the overall design. Has the maker achieved a consistent and balanced statement with his or her handling of shapes, lines, color, texture, and figure? In other words, do you like the way the whole thing looks?

MAKER: Jim Galileo

> *"It's a personal and often expensive undertaking, so you need to like the artist. Do you want to sit at a desk made by someone you don't like?"*
>
> MICHAEL GLOOR, PEACE DALE, R.I.

Getting Down to Business

Certainly, in many cases, it isn't possible to visit the maker's shop, but if the driving distances aren't excessive, consider making the trip. You'll get a better sense of the kind of work done by an individual maker by visiting that person in his or her own work space, particularly if you have the opportunity to see work in progress. And a little one-on-one conversation in the craftsman's shop can go a long way toward determining your compatibility with that maker. You don't have to establish a friendship with the individual who builds your custom furniture, although that may happen, but you do have to feel comfortable enough with that person to trust him to deliver a piece of furniture capable of providing you with years of service and pleasure.

MAKER: **Stephen Smith**

MAKER: **Christoph Neander**

The creation of good custom furniture requires good communication. It is a collaborative effort in which the needs and tastes of the client come together with the experience and tastes of the craftsman to produce furniture that couldn't have existed if either party had been absent from the process. So don't be reluctant to contribute. You should be as clear as possible about your expectations.

Share the fruits of your research. Show the maker any sketches, photos, or descriptions that will help you articulate what you feel the piece should be both in terms of function and design, then listen to the craftsman. Furniture design is his or her area of expertise, so that craftsman will be able to offer insights into the design process that can forestall problems before they occur.

At some point, as your thinking about the proposed furniture becomes clearer, the craftsman will develop drawings. These drawings, along with verbal descriptions, will become the plans from which the craftsman develops a price and, if you approve that price, the finished piece. So it is therefore imperative that you study these drawings and pay attention to the descriptions so that you understand exactly what it is that you may be buying.

Early in this collaborative planning process, you may choose to speak with the craftsman about price. Such a discussion could be useful if you have a spending limit

you're unwilling to exceed. Don't be surprised, however, if the craftsman is unwilling to offer a ball-park figure. He or she may justifiably feel reluctant to offer a guess until all the details of the design and construction processes have been articulated and agreed upon. Just remember that in most cases, you will be asked to pay for designs and estimates even if you don't choose to buy the piece under consideration. This is true even though many craftsmen roll the design costs into the purchase price for clients who do, in fact, make the proposed purchase.

MAKER:
Gregory Vasileff

If you've paid close attention throughout the planning process, there shouldn't be any surprises when it comes time to review the contract your craftsman has prepared. Read that document carefully. Make sure it includes detailed specifications and accurate drawings. Also make sure that the contract designates a mutually agreeable completion date.

In addition, the contract should spell out the schedule of payments. Different craftsmen approach this issue in different ways, but virtually all will expect some money at signing—often 50%. Many contracts will request that the balance be made in one more payment, due on delivery of the finished piece. However, some craftsmen prefer a schedule of three or four payments spread out over the construction process, particularly if the order is very large and complex.

Finally, you should discuss the shipping process. As you'll see from reading the entries in this book, many craftsmen offer free local delivery but charge extra for crating and long-distance shipping.

When the drawings, specifications, and contractual terms are clear and agreeable to both parties, it's time to sign the contract.

"Be open to listening to the craftsman because—if you have picked right—he has the aesthetic vocabulary and construction experience to foresee potential pitfalls, as well as visualize the beauty."

SCOTT ERNST, GLORIETA, N. MEX.

MAKER: John Houck

MAKER: Timothy Philbrick

The Waiting Game

Once the contract is signed, the hard part begins: waiting. As you'll see by reading this book, top-level craftsmen schedule their work months (or even years) in advance. In fact, once a contract has been signed, it might be months before work even begins on the piece you've ordered, and then additional weeks or months will pass before the piece is in your hands.

You may have some contact with the craftsman during this time. He or she may call to discuss material purchase or to nail down a detail that was not specified in the contract, but if you make frequent calls to check on the status of your job in the queue or just to chat about the progress of the job, you're robbing that craftsman of time needed in the construction process.

Remember, too, that any changes you may request in the design at this stage will probably necessitate an increase in cost to cover the extra material and labor required by that change. This can be true even for changes that appear to be very minor.

Be patient. Allow the process to unfold. Trust the craftsman. Trust the judgment you displayed in selecting that craftsman. Although waiting can be difficult, the potential rewards are enormous.

STEPS FOR BUYING CUSTOM FURNITURE

1 Research the piece you wish to buy.

2 Research potential makers.

3 Select a maker.

4 Discuss the necessary features—size, configuration, materials, style—with that maker.

5 Discuss the construction schedule, payment schedule, and shipping arrangements.

6 Sign a contract in which the above elements have been clearly expressed.

Aequalis Furniture

"To keep craft in woodworking from slipping away, we have made every effort to build pieces that are uncompromising in their attention to detail and execution."

ACCORDING TO TOM HOBGOOD, a piece of sleek, modern furniture is more demanding than its classical counterpart in at least one important respect: It gives the furniture maker no moldings to hide behind. This suits Hobgood just fine. In fact, he sees an opportunity in the demands modern furniture places on the contemporary craftsman—an opportunity to maintain high standards of craftsmanship in the midst of a culture in which these standards appear to be sinking into the ground.

Although the designs he builds are clearly very modern (he often combines wood and metal in strikingly nontraditional ways), Hobgood relies on time-tested traditional joinery—hand-cut dovetails, for example—to give his pieces strength and durability.

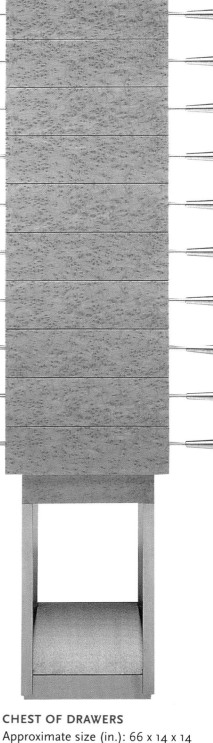

DETAIL

CHEST OF DRAWERS
Approximate size (in.): 66 x 14 x 14
Materials: maple, stainless steel, glass

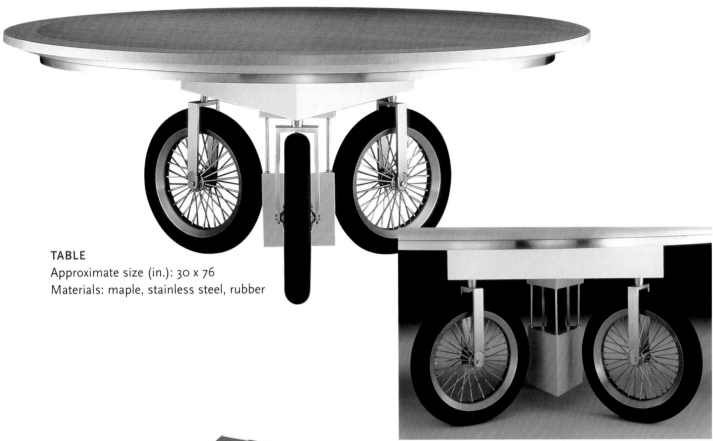

TABLE
Approximate size (in.): 30 x 76
Materials: maple, stainless steel, rubber

DETAIL

TABLES
Approximate sizes (in.): 24 x 24 x 24, 24 x 17 x 26
Materials: maple, stainless steel, glass

Tom Hobgood
2426 Dunavant St.
Charlotte, NC 28203
(704) 344-1112
FAX (704) 344-1264
THobgood@aequalisfurniture.com
www.aequalisfurniture.com

DESIGN CHARGES:	$50 per hour rolled into purchase price
DEPOSIT:	50% with balance due on completion
LEAD TIME:	1½–2 months
LOCAL DELIVERY:	free
LONG DISTANCE:	inquire

Alexious Designs Associates

"The Ming period of Chinese furniture produced excellent examples of both joinery and elegant design, which makes that furniture appropriate for any interior."

RANDOLPH DEMERCADO became a furniture maker because he couldn't find the right kind of table on which to place the bonsai trees he was culturing. He did find drawings of such tables in Gustav Eckes's book *Domestic Chinese Furniture,* so after studying the book, he began to build tables patterned after those drawings. At first he built only for himself, but then he began building for other members of his bonsai club, and finally in 1987 he left his day job to become a full-time furniture maker, specializing in Ming dynasty reproductions.

DeMercado is particularly drawn to the joinery of the furniture he reproduces, which is quite unlike that of traditional Western furniture. He is fascinated by its intricacies, and he has great respect for its ability to hold furniture together over several centuries.

DeMercado's work has appeared on the pages of a number of magazines, including *Traditional Home, Home Furniture,* and *Fine Woodworking.*

ARMCHAIR
Approximate size (in.): 21 x 25 x 19
Material: padauk

SOFA TABLE
Approximate size (in.): 32 x 71 x 21
Material: padauk

PSALTERY TABLE
Approximate size (in.): 34 x 57 x 16
Material: rosewood

DETAIL

SIDE TABLE
Approximate size (in.): 22 x 29 x 24
Material: spalted maple

Randolph A. DeMercado
20 Blue Spruce Trail
Warwick, NY 10990
(845) 986-2815
FAX (845) 986-2815

DESIGN CHARGES:	none
DEPOSIT:	50% with balance due on delivery
LEAD TIME:	3 months
LOCAL DELIVERY:	at cost
LONG DISTANCE:	best available shipper, no crating charge

Om Anand

"The energy that goes into the making emanates upon completion."

OM ANAND trained with Makoto Imai, a Japanese temple builder, and at The College of the Redwoods with James Krenov. This background has enabled Anand to approach his craft with a thorough grounding in essential technical skills combined with a spiritual aim. It is his reverence for the process as well as the materials and the product that draws him to clients who want personalized service. He uses a combination of solid woods and shop-sawn veneers. In particular, he is drawn to certain local woods not available through commercial outlets.

Although Anand does sometimes sell through galleries, most of his work is done as commissions earned through positive word of mouth. Several of his pieces appear in James Krenov's book, *With Wakened Hands* (Cambium Press, 2000).

FOOTSTOOL
Approximate size (in.): 16 x 18 x 11
Material: Douglas fir

CASE-ON-CASE
Approximate size (in.): 81 x 26 x 22
Material: walnut

RELIQUARY
Approximate size (in.): 11 x 6 x 6
Materials: kwila, cypress

CASE-ON-CASE
Approximate size (in.): 71 x 43 x 19
Materials: bird's-eye maple, walnut

3731 Paul Sweet Rd.
Santa Cruz, CA 95065
(831) 479-3590

DESIGN CHARGES:	$250 rolled into purchase price
DEPOSIT:	50% with balance due on completion
LEAD TIME:	6 months
LOCAL DELIVERY:	free
LONG DISTANCE:	best available shipper, plus crating charge

Andy Rae Woodworking and Writing Studios

"My work is more than just a business: It's a very personal expression of who I am."

ANDY RAE believes that good furniture should be both personal and inviting. To achieve these qualities, he strives to keep his work simple so that his energies can be invested in the details. Silhouetted lightning bolts etched onto a painted surface, hand-carved door pulls, and custom moldings all add a personal touch.

Rae prepared for a career as a furniture maker by apprenticing with several outstanding designers/craftsmen including Frank Klausz and George Nakashima. Then 15 years ago he set out on his own, quickly earning a reputation as an accomplished furniture maker.

He is the author of several books on woodworking, as well as many magazine articles. He has taught at woodworking schools all over the country and has also been the producer of two woodworking videos and a guest on a number of TV programs.

WINE CABINET
Approximate size (in.): 40 x 60 x 16
Materials: anigre, mahogany, marble

LIGHTNING CHEST
Approximate size (in.): 26 x 47 x 22
Materials: sugar pine, walnut

RIGHT CABINET
Approximate size (in.): 120 x 108 x 24
Materials: sugar pine, mahogany,
plywood, glass, brass

HALL TABLE
Approximate size (in.): 34 x 144 x 16
Materials: mahogany, MDF, brass

35 Sunrise Valley
Leicester, NC 28748
(828) 683-0683
FAX(828) 683-5300
Woodrae@aol.com

DESIGN CHARGES:	$200+ rolled into purchase price
DEPOSIT:	20% with balance due on completion
LEAD TIME:	2–6 months
LOCAL DELIVERY:	$150+
LONG DISTANCE:	best available shipper, plus crating charge (minimum $100)

Antique Refinishers

"I have never owned a table saw and make my living entirely by hand."

W. PATRICK EDWARDS modestly observes that he has a lot of patience. Unquestionably, the proof of that patience is written on every marquetried surface that leaves his shop.

Edwards is a self-taught cabinet-maker, but he has received instruction in early 19th-century furniture characteristics at the Winterthur Summer Institute, as well as instruction in 18th-century French marquetry, cabinetmaking, and finishing at Ecole Boulle in Paris. In 2000, Edwards established The American School of French Marquetry.

Last year, after 30 years of focusing on re-creating pre-industrial furniture, Edwards began producing contemporary designs.

Edwards's work has appeared in many juried exhibitions, frequently taking top honors. He has also been the subject of many newspaper and magazine articles, including a cover story in *Woodwork* magazine. In 1973, he researched and wrote a five-hour CBS television series entitled *Welcome to the Past: The History of American Furniture.*

ROCKE TABLE
Approximate size (in.): 28 x 24 x 24
Materials: pewter, purpleheart, aluminum

BONHEUR DU JOUR LADY'S DESK
Approximate size (in.): 41 x 29 x 20
Materials: mahogany, oak bronze, marble,
    brass, leather

BUTTERFLY CENTER TABLE
Approximate size (in.): 31 x 36 x 36
Materials: various

W. Patrick Edwards
3815 Utah St.
San Diego, CA 92104
(619) 298-0864
FAX (619) 297-0500
ebeniste@pacbell.net
www.wpatrickedwards.com

DESIGN CHARGES:	included in 50% deposit
DEPOSIT:	50% with balance due on completion
LEAD TIME:	2–6 months
LOCAL DELIVERY:	free in Southern California
LONG DISTANCE:	best available shipper, plus crating charge

Art Forms Furniture

"Although function sometimes plays a secondary role in my work, it is important for me to join my ideas and inspirations with a usable everyday object."

CHRIS MARTIN approaches woodworking from the perspective of an artist. Although his work is functional, it is also intended to challenge traditional notions of what furniture can be. He enjoys the exploration of new materials and techniques, which has led him to incorporate steel and concrete (and many other exotic materials) into his furniture. He prides himself on creating pieces that are "completely unique."

His preparation as a furniture maker began when he earned a B.F.A. from Iowa State University, which he followed with an M.F.A. in furniture design from the Rhode Island School of Design. He currently serves on the faculty of Iowa State University, where he teaches several wood-design classes.

CURIO CABINET
Approximate size (in.): 81 x 30 x 26
Materials: olive-ash burl, ash, basswood, silverleaf

CHEST OF DRAWERS
Approximate size (in.): 60 x 52 x 21
Materials: quilted maple, chechen, curly maple, forged steel

MEDIA CABINET
Approximate size (in.): 44 x 45 x 27
Materials: bird's-eye redwood, catspaw cherry,
white oak, steel, bronze

BENCH
Approximate size (in.): 24 x 74 x 30
Materials: redwood, steel, concrete

Chris Martin
1512 Florida Ave.
Ames, IA 50014
(515) 268-9343
FAX (515) 268-9343
chmartin@iastate.edu

DESIGN CHARGES:	$48 per hour rolled into purchase price
DEPOSIT:	50% with balance due on completion
LEAD TIME:	2½–3 months
LOCAL DELIVERY:	free
LONG DISTANCE:	best available shipper, plus crating charge

Lonnie Bird

"My business is distinctive because of the furniture I produce. I'm uncompromising on the details that set my work apart. I'm never satisfied until each element of a design works with the entire piece."

LONNIE BIRD stresses the importance of "lines, details, and proportions" in the furniture that leaves his shop in northeastern Tennessee. For Bird, the design process includes the construction of prototypes he uses for study and evaluation. Then once he has resolved any problems in the overall design, he turns his attention to the details.

He sees the immaculate execution of every aspect of the furniture maker's craft as critical. "The curve of an arm, the fit of a drawer, and the color of a finish all play a role in the success of a piece of furniture," Bird explains.

Bird began his career as a furniture maker the old-fashioned way, by apprenticing in a four-year program, before setting out on his own. During his distinguished 22-year career, he has been recognized several times by *Early American Life* magazine as one of the United States's best craftsmen.

DETAIL

DESK AND BOOKCASE
Approximate size (in.): 95 x 38 x 22
Material: walnut

DETAIL

CORNER CABINET
Approximate size (in.): 87 x 42 x 20
Materials: walnut, poplar

CARVED ARMCHAIR
Approximate size (in.): 41 x 24 x 20
Material: walnut

1145 Carolina Dr.
Dandridge, TN 37725
www.lonniebird.com

DESIGN CHARGES:	percentage of sale
DEPOSIT:	50% with balance due on completion
LEAD TIME:	8 months
LOCAL DELIVERY:	time and mileage
LONG DISTANCE:	inquire

Black Creek Designs, LLC

"Together, my clients and I define the parameters that the design of a piece is to fulfill. These parameters are often springboards for new ideas and forms."

ALLURED BY THE ROMANCE of the workshop and the richness of wood, Thomas Throop decided to become a maker of fine furniture several years after receiving a B.A. in economics from Connecticut College. His preparation for his new career began at the John Makepeace School for Craftsmen in Wood in Dorset, England, where he learned the traditions of fine craftsmanship and the skillful use of hand tools, knowledge that informs every piece that leaves his shop.

Throop designs furniture that is "simple, honest, and direct." He achieves this by creating "elegance informed by design: a harmonious play of line, proportion, surface, and space. I strive for visually strong and confident forms that maintain a delicate, airy, and open quality."

Throop's work has appeared in dozens of exhibitions in the northeastern United States, as well as in several shows in England. His work has been featured in a number of publications, including *Home Furniture* and *House and Garden*.

FISHERS ISLAND SCREEN
Approximate size (in.): 63 x 55 x 14
Materials: walnut, curly maple, redwood burl

MARIANNE AND LEONARD'S SOFA
Approximate size (in.): 33 x 64 x 27
Materials: walnut, upholstery

HEAD-OF-HARBOR JEWELRY CABINET
Approximate size (in.): 72 x 44 x 18
Materials: walnut, claro walnut, mahogany, bog oak

FARM-CREEK SIDE TABLES
Approximate size (in.): 24 x 18 x 18 (each)
Materials: walnut, oak burl

Thomas Throop
345 Wilson Ave.
Norwalk, CT 06854
(203) 855-9334
FAX (203) 855-9334
tom@blackcreekdesigns.com
www.blackcreekdesigns.com

DESIGN CHARGES:	5%–10% rolled into purchase price
DEPOSIT:	50% with balance due on completion
LEAD TIME:	4–6 months
LOCAL DELIVERY:	inquire
LONG DISTANCE:	best available shipper, plus crating charge of $50 per hour plus materials

Blackwater Woodworks

"Furniture at this level is a craft, not a commodity."

R. A. LAUFER builds furniture the way he likes it built: by hand, one piece at a time, with enough subtle differences in each so that no two pieces are exactly alike. Working alone in his Baltimore shop, he crafts his furniture from domestic hardwoods, mostly cherry, walnut, and maple, frequently using figured varieties of these species. He prefers exposed joinery and a hand-rubbed mixture of oil and varnish finish.

Laufer's designs are original, but he acknowledges an aesthetic debt to the American Shakers, to postwar Danish designers, as well as to contemporary designers/craftsmen such as Sam Maloof and George Nakashima.

Although Laufer has been a professional furniture maker for only two years, his work has appeared in nearly a dozen juried shows, as well as in a half-dozen publications, including *Fine Woodworking* and *Woodshop News.*

SIDE CHAIR
Approximate size (in.): 37 x 20 x 23
Material: cherry

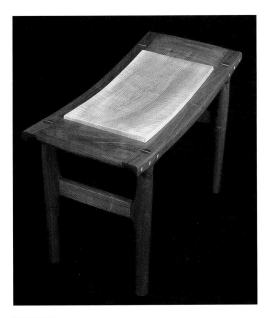

BENCH
Approximate size (in.): 18 x 29 x 14
Materials: walnut, curly maple

TABLE
Approximate size (in.): 30 x 28
Materials: bird's-eye maple,
    curly maple

DESK
Approximate size (in.): 30 x 47 x 26
Material: walnut

R. A. Laufer
712 Winans Way
Baltimore, MD 21229
(410) 362-3755
FAX (410) 362-3755
ralaufer@blackwaterwoodworks.com
www.blackwaterwoodworks.com

DESIGN CHARGES:	none
DEPOSIT:	50% with balance due on completion
LEAD TIME:	3–9 months
LOCAL DELIVERY:	free
LONG DISTANCE:	blanket-wrap shipper

Bob Kopf's Wooden Works

"I avoid decoration and strive for strong, clear forms and simple lines."

SUCCESSFUL CRAFTSMEN design to take maximum advantage of their personal strengths. In Bob Kopf's case, his work features surfaces created using hand-planes: "All edges, forms, and surfaces are planed to shape, capturing human energy and vitalizing the finished piece."

This approach not only impacts the finished surfaces he creates but also affects the way Kopf thinks about the processes of working wood. Since hand-plane usage requires following grain direction, he has learned to design and work in sympathy with his raw material.

Kopf specializes in solid-wood construction using traditional joinery. He prefers domestic species, but he does sometimes use "eco-approved imports." He applies a variety of finishes, including oil, oil/varnish, wax, and polyurethane.

His work has appeared in dozens of juried exhibits throughout the eastern United States, including four one-man shows. His work has also appeared in many publications.

LIBRARY LADDER
Approximate size (in.): 76 x 22 x 26
Materials: walnut, curly maple

BAMBOO TABLES

Approximate sizes (in.): 42 x 13 x 13, 24 x 13 x 13,
36 x 24 x 13
Materials: mahogany, teak

HALL TREES

Approximate sizes (in.): 68–70 x 12–14
Materials: various

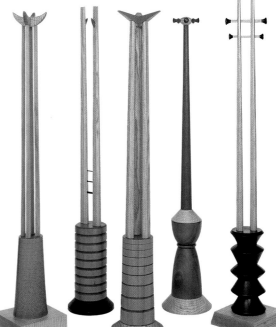

TABLE

Approximate size (in.): 29 x 42 x 42
Materials: cherry, spalted curly maple

1115 Dodson Ridge Rd.
Walnut Cove, NC 27052
(336) 591-4973
bobkopfww@msn.com

DESIGN CHARGES:	$150+ rolled into purchase price
DEPOSIT:	33%–50% with balance due on completion
LEAD TIME:	6–9 months
LOCAL DELIVERY:	free for delivery within 4 hours of shop
LONG DISTANCE:	best available shipper, plus crating charge

Boston Woodworking Co. Ltd.

"The synthesis of 18th-century technique and form with contemporary material and design attracts clients to my work."

ALTHOUGH MARK ARNOLD feels at home working in nearly any furniture genre, he is drawn to Federal forms and motifs. In this style, he uses highly figured veneers, which allow him to be creative with texture and color.

Arnold makes exact replicas of specific Federal originals, but he prefers to reinterpret those originals in a contemporary way. He enjoys taking traditional techniques and forms and changing them by using veneer that an earlier craftsman would not have had, or by changing the shape in a way that makes the piece contemporary but still inspired by our furniture-making predecessors."

Arnold has been profiled in *Woodwork* magazine, and his work has appeared in other publications, including the *Washington Post*. He has exhibited in many juried regional shows, taking home Best of Show awards at the Artistry in Wood show in Dayton, Ohio, and the Findlay Area Arts Festival.

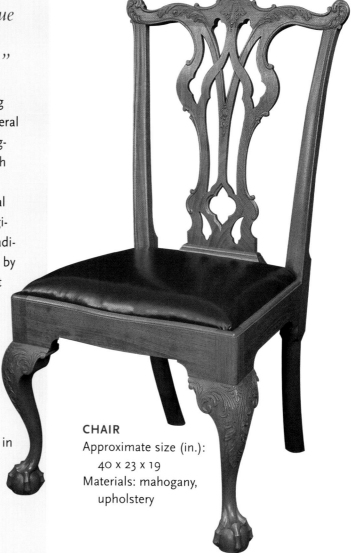

CHAIR
Approximate size (in.):
40 x 23 x 19
Materials: mahogany,
upholstery

DEMILUNE TABLES
Approximate size (in.): 30 x 39 x 20
Materials: many woods, including
mahogany, avodire

DEMILUNE TABLE
Approximate size (in.): 29 x 30 x 13
Materials: walnut, bubinga, holly, ebony

CHAIR
Approximate size (in.): 40 x 22 x 18
Materials: mahogany, upholstery

Mark Arnold
423A S. Galena Rd.
Sunbury, OH 43074
(740) 965-9618
FAX (740) 965-6708
bostonww.@aol.com
www.bostonwoodworking.com

DESIGN CHARGES:	$150 rolled into purchase price
DEPOSIT:	50% with balance due on completion
LEAD TIME:	4–6 months
LOCAL DELIVERY:	free
LONG DISTANCE:	best available shipper, plus crating charge

James Bowie

"Classical furniture has retained its presence for more than 300 years. With regard to conservation and design, it speaks for itself."

JAMES BOWIE prides himself on being able to provide his clients with antiques designed to function in contemporary homes, at prices substantially less than the original antiques. He believes the antiques he creates would have been seen, stylistically, as "on the edge" during the 17th and 18th centuries.

Born and raised in Glasgow, Scotland, Bowie received his training through a four-year apprenticeship in Europe, followed by three years of study at a woodworking college. He came to America in 1992, setting up shop in Fort Bragg, California. There Bowie builds his furniture primarily of solid wood, using the same techniques as the period masters he emulates. This is work he has done for more than 25 years.

His work has appeared at the Laguna Beach Festival of the Arts, as well as in the San Francisco Design Center. He has written several articles for *Woodwork West*.

ROBERT ADAM DEMILUNE CABINET
Approximate size (in.): 33 x 50 x 24
Materials: satinwood, maple, various other woods in marquetry

TABLE AND CHAIRS
Approximate size (in.):
30 x 52 x 120 (table)
Material: mahogany

ARMCHAIR
Approximate size (in.): 39 x 27 x 25
Material: mahogany

TABLE AND CHAIRS
Approximate size (in.): 30 x 54 x 186 (table)
Materials: satinwood, walnut

541 S. Franklin St.
Fort Bragg, CA 95437
(707) 964-8798
FAX (707) 964-8798
jbowie@mcn.org
www.jamesbowie.com

DESIGN CHARGES:	$250 rolled into purchase price
DEPOSIT:	25% with balance paid in stages
LEAD TIME:	6 months
LOCAL DELIVERY:	$50 per hour, plus gas
LONG DISTANCE:	best available shipper, plus crating charge

Bradley A. Boggie, Furnituremaker

"I believe that my personal investment in each piece ensures that the outcome is of the highest standards."

BRADLEY BOGGIE doesn't confine the work that issues from his San Francisco shop to a single style or period. Instead, he works in many styles, his forms sometimes evoking Federal, Arts and Crafts, Art Deco, and other themes. He believes this eclectic approach to design is essential if he is to meet the needs of a diverse clientele.

Boggie prefers traditional joinery, employing dovetail and mortise-and-tenon construction techniques. He then creates the final surfaces using handplanes, scrapers, and sandpaper. Although he works primarily with solid woods, he does make occasional use of veneer to highlight panels, tabletops, and drawer fronts.

His work has appeared in galleries throughout Northern California, including the International Airport Museum Gallery in San Francisco.

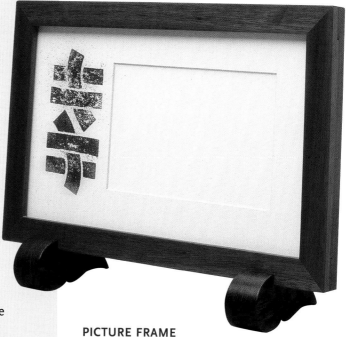

PICTURE FRAME
Approximate size (in.): 10 x 15 x 3
Materials: bloodwood, wenge

HUMIDOR
Approximate size (in.): 8 x 22 x 14
Materials: katalox, Spanish cedar

ATLAS STAND
Approximate size (in.): 32 x 28 x 18
Materials: granadillo, sycamore

CONFERENCE TABLE
Approximate size (in.): 30 x 120 x 48
Materials: kwilla, zebrawood

2415 Third St., No. 242
San Francisco, CA 94107
(415) 503-0967
bboggie@earthlink.net

DESIGN CHARGES:	inquire
DEPOSIT:	50% with balance due on completion
LEAD TIME:	1½–2 months
LOCAL DELIVERY:	inquire
LONG DISTANCE:	inquire

Brian Jones Woodworking

"My work is not repetitive, and I try to challenge and expand my skills by exploring new styles or techniques with each project."

BRIAN JONES takes pride in his ability to give concrete form to the wishes of his clients. Working in a variety of styles, Jones collaborates with his clients to create designs that reflect their "unique tastes and needs in a quality, high-end product." He produces original designs as well as pieces inspired by past masters.

Jones constructs the furniture using traditional wood-to-wood joinery and a mixture of solid woods and exotic veneers. He completes the pieces with either a sprayed lacquer or hand-rubbed oil finish.

His work has appeared in a juried show at the Vermont State Craft Center at Frog Hollow. He has also shown his work at many other galleries in his home state, including the Vermont State Craft Centers in Burlington, Middlebury, Windsor, and Manchester.

ARMOIRE
Approximate size (in.): 78 x 37 x 18
Materials: walnut, ebony

TABLE
Approximate size (in.): 32 x 72 x 14
Material: mahogany

CHAIRS
Approximate size (in.): 38 x 22 x 20
Materials: walnut, quilted maple

SIDEBOARD
Approximate size (in.): 36 x 72 x 18
Materials: quilted maple, walnut, ebony

73 Highlands Dr.
Williston, VT 05495
(802) 878-4895
FAX (802) 872-8661
bjoneswd@together.net
www.together.net/~bjoneswd

DESIGN CHARGES:	$38 per hour rolled into purchase price
DEPOSIT:	33%, plus 33% in progress, with balance due on completion
LEAD TIME:	2–3 months
LOCAL DELIVERY:	free
LONG DISTANCE:	best available shipper, plus blanket-wrap charge

Curtis Buchanan

"I design chairs in an organic, seat-of-the-pants way. I feel more comfortable drilling holes in boards to see how spindles should be placed rather than drawing them on paper."

ALTHOUGH CURTIS BUCHANAN has a deep affection for the Windsor chair as an object, he makes his living as a chairmaker because he loves the process of constructing that object. "Even the most mundane of tasks, that of whittling the spindles with a drawknife, has its beauty," he explains. "Its repetition has the magic of meditation where concentration is broken down to single cuts of the knife, and finished products are those cuts themselves."

He identifies three major influences on his approach to his craft. The first is a local cabinetmaker, Hugh Bowman, whose work ethic Buchanan admires. The second is chairmaker Dave Sawyer (see p. 64), from whom Buchanan learned the importance of the unstinting pursuit of quality. And the third is chairmaker Brian Boggs of Berea, Kentucky. From Boggs, Buchanan learned to view his work each day with a fresh and critical eye.

Buchanan's work has appeared in a number of books and magazines. He has also been commissioned three times to create chairs for Monticello, the home of Thomas Jefferson.

BIRDCAGE WINDSOR
Approximate size (in.): 37 x 17 x 17
Materials: pine, maple, oak

SIDE CHAIR
Approximate size (in.): 39 x 18 x 17
Materials: poplar, maple, oak

SACKBACK SETTEE
Approximate size (in.): 38 x 40 x 16
Materials: pine, maple, oak

WRITING ARMCHAIR
Approximate size (in.): 46 x 32 x 30
Materials: various woods

208 E. Main St.
Jonesborough, TN 37659
(423) 753-5160
buchanan357@aol.com

DESIGN CHARGES:	inquire
DEPOSIT:	20% with balance due on completion
LEAD TIME:	6–24 months
LOCAL DELIVERY:	free
LONG DISTANCE:	motor freight or UPS, plus $50–$60 crating charge

Charles Durfee, Cabinetmaker

"My business approach is plain and simple. The work and the many satisfied customers speak for themselves."

CHARLES DURFEE doesn't try to make a statement with his work. He strives, instead, to create furniture that is quiet, elegant, and personal. His furniture emulates that created by the early New England craftsmen, whose work originally set Durfee on his course as a furniture maker.

Durfee uses machines for the brute work of ripping and planing, but his joinery is cut by hand and his surfaces are created using planes and scrapers. Like his predecessors, Durfee works in domestic species, primarily cherry, walnut, and maple, finishing those materials with oil, varnish, shellac, or lacquer.

Durfee's work has appeared in many galleries and exhibitions throughout New England. His work has also been selected several times to appear in *Early American Homes Directory of Traditional American Crafts*.

STOOL
Approximate size (in.): 36 x 17 x 14
Material: cherry

SOFA
Approximate size (in.): 34 x 72 x 32
Materials: cherry, upholstery

COLLECTOR'S CABINET
Approximate size (in.): 36 x 24 x 18
Materials: cherry, curly cherry

65 Delano Rd.
Woolwich, ME 04579
(207) 442-7049
cdurfee@gwi.net
www.cdurfee.com

DESIGN CHARGES:	$30 per hour rolled into purchase price
DEPOSIT:	50% with balance due on completion
LEAD TIME:	3–6 months
LOCAL DELIVERY:	approximately 10% of purchase price
LONG DISTANCE:	blanket-wrap shipper or UPS, plus crating charge

C. H. Becksvoort Furniture Maker

"My aim is to build the highest-quality, individually built furniture. Toward that end, I use the best sustainably harvested cherry, nontoxic finishes, and time-honored techniques of joinery and craftsmanship."

FOR MORE THAN 20 YEARS, Chris Becksvoort has done restoration work for the Shaker community at Sabbathday Lake. It's not surprising then that he identifies Shaker furniture as the most potent design influence in his furniture-making life.

Like the Shakers before him, Becksvoort works with domestic woods and a combination of hand and power tools. With these materials and tools, he produces a line of furniture that he guarantees for the life of the client. This reflects not only Becksvoort's belief in the enduring quality of his own work but also his belief in the inherent value of good furniture, regardless of the maker. "A well-designed, well-built piece of furniture that lasts 100 years is preferable to one bought at a quarter of the price but which must be replaced every 10 years," he says.

His work has appeared in galleries and museums in Maine and Massachusetts, as well as in the Smithsonian Craft Show in Washington, D.C. He is the author of *The Shaker Legacy* (The Taunton Press, 1998).

TALL CABINET
Approximate size (in.):
79 x 18 x 13
Material: cherry

WORK COUNTER
Approximate size (in.): 36 x 72 x 24
Material: cherry

HANGING LAMP
Approximate size (in.): 12 x 17 x 17
Material: birch

FLOOR LAMP
Approximate size (in.): 60 x 18 x 18
Materials: fir, cherry

15-DRAWER CHEST
Approximate size (in.): 50 x 15 x 14
Material: cherry

Chris Becksvoort
P. O. Box 12
New Gloucester, ME 04260
(207) 926-4608
www.chbecksvoort.com

DESIGN CHARGES:	$100 minimum rolled into purchase price
DEPOSIT:	50% with balance due on completion
LEAD TIME:	6–18 months
LOCAL DELIVERY:	free in Maine
LONG DISTANCE:	best available shipper, plus crating charge

Christoph Neander: Art and Design in Fine Furniture

"It is no coincidence that I have chosen to live and work among the arid lands and open spaces of the American Southwest, where the beauty of natural forms and colors are not subdued, but rather enhanced, by the lack of visual distractions."

WHEN CHRISTOPH NEANDER builds furniture, he searches for a "sense of timeless elegance," which he seeks to achieve through understatement. To reflect the subtle contrasts of his arid Southwest landscape, he uses a variety of materials, textures, and colors and juxtaposes sensuous curves and cold, hard materials. He compares his work to a plainly written but riveting story with an "interesting plot twist" as opposed to a story told with "the beauty of flowery verse."

His training combines a formal four-year apprenticeship in his native Germany with an informal 16-year study of contemporary design aesthetics. This background has prepared him to create furniture that is both grounded in tradition and contemporary in appeal.

Neander's work has appeared in shows sponsored by the Smithsonian, the Rhode Island School of Design, and the Architect and Design Building in New York. In 1999, he won a fellowship grant from the Colorado Council of Arts. Also that year, he was an Artist in Residence at the Anderson Ranch Arts Center in Snowmass, Colorado.

CABINET
Approximate size (in.): 74 x 40 x 20
Materials: Douglas fir, maple

TV CABINET

Approximate size (in.): 67 x 41 x 24
Materials: bird's-eye maple, black walnut

COFFEE TABLE

Approximate size (in.): 18 x 47 x 37
Materials: curly maple, maple

CHEST OF DRAWERS

Approximate size (in.): 58 x 23 x 23
Material: ash

2214 W. Alameda St., Unit A
Santa Fe, NM 87501
(505) 471-0534
FAX (505) 471-0534
c_neander@hotmail.com

DESIGN CHARGES:	initial design session free, subsequent design time $40 per hour rolled into purchase price
DEPOSIT:	33%, 33% due mid-project, balance due on completion
LEAD TIME:	2–6 months
LOCAL DELIVERY:	free
LONG DISTANCE:	common carrier, plus crating charge

Claire Fruitman Furnituremaking

"It is my goal in my work to find the place where art meets craft, a place where I use traditional techniques to make a contemporary piece, a place where I design fine enough work to be called an artist and use fine enough skills to be called a craftsman."

CLAIRE FRUITMAN strives to combine artistry and craftsmanship in every piece that leaves her shop. To do so, she likes to use the full range of traditional skills she acquired during her two-year program at the North Bennet Street School in Boston.

Fruitman has taught woodworking throughout the Boston area, including at the North Bennet Street School. She was also a panelist for the Furniture Society's "Women in Woodworking: Issues and Answers" conference held in San Francisco in 1998. Her work has appeared on the pages of *Furniture Studio: The Heart of the Functional Arts* (Cambium Press, 1999), as well as in several magazines, including *British House and Garden* and *American Woodworker*.

CHEST
Approximate size (in.): 17 x 8 x 6
Materials: spalted maple, ebony

CHEST OF DRAWERS
Approximate size (in.): 39 x 24 x 12
Materials: maple, plywood, brass

TABLE
Approximate size (in.): 30 x 30 x 15
Material: mahogany

DETAIL

368 Congress St., 4th Fl.
Boston, MA 02210
(617) 338-9487
fruitman@hotmail.com

DESIGN CHARGES:	inquire
DEPOSIT:	inquire
LEAD TIME:	inquire
LOCAL DELIVERY:	inquire
LONG DISTANCE:	inquire

Bruce Cohen

"If you are confident that the woodworker understands what you want, that there is a price you can both live with, and that you trust his or her integrity, artistry, and chemistry, then the result is bound to be good."

AFTER BEGINNING HIS WORKING LIFE as a jeweler, Bruce Cohen became a self-taught furniture maker. He didn't completely leave behind his first career, though. He took into his woodworking shop many of the design motifs he had originally forged in gold and silver.

Cohen describes his work as often being "sculptural" and "sometimes delicate," but he takes pains to construct his work so that it will withstand the rigors of normal use and abuse. To achieve this durability, he relies on domestic hardwoods and uses traditional mortise-and-tenon joinery.

Cohen explains that it isn't necessary for prospective clients to bring him a completed design, a difficult endeavor for many nondesigners. "I have 30 years of design experience, and it's usually my job to confront the blank paper." If the client knows what he wants, though, Cohen is happy to work from a client's design.

COFFEE TABLE
Approximate size (in.): 17 x 36 x 36
Materials: cherry, glass

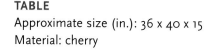

TABLE
Approximate size (in.): 36 x 40 x 15
Material: cherry

WRITING DESK
Approximate size (in.): 30 x 56 x 24
Materials: cherry, walnut

CHAIR
Approximate size (in.): 36 x 19 x 19
Material: cherry

DISPLAY CASE
Approximate size (in.): 71 x 37 x 14
Materials: walnut, glass

4949 N. Broadway #140
Boulder, CO 80304
(303) 440-4838
FAX (303) 440-6052
bruce@boulder.net
www.brucecohen.com

DESIGN CHARGES: inquire
DEPOSIT: 50% with balance due
on completion
LEAD TIME: 2–10 months
LOCAL DELIVERY: free
LONG DISTANCE: inquire

Colorado Colonial Furniture

"I get great pleasure in adapting 18th-century style to more modern applications and seeing customers' pleasure at the completion of a concept that agrees with their notion of style."

ROBERT HODGETTS knew at an early age that he wanted to build functional, long-lasting art. His fascination with wood grain and figure combined with his mother's interest in antiques led him to become a furniture maker. And once Hodgetts made his first cabriole leg, he knew he had found his niche in the fluid lines of 18th-century furniture.

Some of his works accurately replicate particular 18th-century examples, while others are adaptations that are designed to meet the needs of 21st-century clients. Like his 18th-century mentors, Hodgetts builds in mahogany, cherry, walnut, and maple, using hand-worked dovetail and mortise-and-tenon joinery. He finishes his work with hand-applied oil and varnish or with shellac and wax preparations.

QUEEN ANNE HIGHBOY
Approximate size (in.): 84 x 40 x 23
Materials: tiger maple, poplar

BALL-AND-CLAW CHEST OF DRAWERS
Approximate size (in.): 32 x 34 x 23
Materials: walnut, poplar

END TABLE
Approximate size (in.): 25 x 14 x 20
Material: mahogany

COMPUTER DESK
Approximate size (in.): 72 x 30 x 86
Materials: walnut, cherry, maple

Robert D. Hodgetts
208 Evening Star Rte.
Boulder, CO 80302
(303) 444-2643

DESIGN CHARGES:	none
DEPOSIT:	30%–50% with balance due on completion
LEAD TIME:	1½–2 months
LOCAL DELIVERY:	free
LONG DISTANCE:	ground transport, plus crating charge

Custom Wood Designs

"I strive to create a balance between functional and aesthetic details, all of which contribute to the success of each individual project."

DEAN JACKSON refuses to confine himself to a single furniture style. If the job requires it, he can create original furniture with a medieval flavor, furniture that evokes the Arts and Crafts movement, or furniture with a contemporary sensibility. He explains his approach to design this way: "Every job is 100% custom. The only catalog I use is my portfolio, which gives clients an idea of the type of work I do and the range of styles possible. I keep an open mind and welcome opportunities to explore new design ideas."

His designs begin with practical considerations: How will the piece be used and where will it be sited. He then turns his attention to aesthetic concerns, bringing the piece to life with hand-carved details, inlays, and original leaded glass designs, all presented in the context of furniture assembled using traditional materials and joinery.

His work has appeared in shows throughout Ontario, winning the Best Display Award at the One of a Kind Show in Toronto, and in many regional, national, and international publications, including *Design Book Seven* (The Taunton Press, 1996).

ENTERTAINMENT CABINET
Approximate size (in.): 76 x 34 x 26
Materials: cherry, wenge

SIDEBOARD
Approximate size (in.): 42 x 60 x 20
Material: narra

HIBACHI TABLE
Approximate size (in.): 24 x 42 x 26
Material: walnut

DAVENPORT DESK
Approximate size (in.): 56 x 36 x 26
Material: mahogany

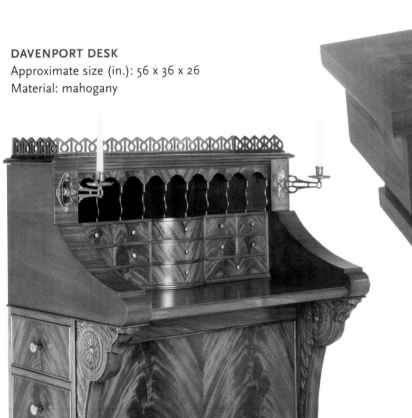

Dean Jackson
45 Brisbane Rd., Unit 6
Toronto, ON M3J 2KL, Canada
(416) 240-1091
FAX (416) 240-9706
deanjackson@look.ca
www.aruacana.com/cwdesigns

DESIGN CHARGES:	$200 (approximately) rolled into purchase price
DEPOSIT:	50% with balance due on completion
LEAD TIME:	4–6 months
LOCAL DELIVERY:	free
LONG DISTANCE:	inquire

Dale Helms Fine Furniture

"The furniture I create reflects my concern for harmony and balance. Subtle details and gentle curves give the eye a pleasant place to rest and explore."

THE FURNITURE THAT DALE HELMS makes does not scream for attention. Instead, he builds furniture that is "good for the long haul; furniture that is quiet, graceful, and pleasing to the eye." In an increasingly hectic world, Helms believes in surrounding ourselves with artifacts imbued with peace and quietude.

Working primarily with solid wood, Helms crafts his pieces by hand, assembling cases using mortise-and-tenon and dovetail construction. He then scrapes the pieces smooth and finishes them with an oil/varnish mix, polished shellac, or occasionally lacquer.

Helms's work has appeared at the ACC Craft Fair in Baltimore, the Philadelphia Furniture and Furnishings Show, as well as many juried exhibitions in Vermont.

COFFEE TABLE
Approximate size (in.): 18 x 30 x 40
Materials: cherry, plywood, tiles
   (custom made by Bonneme Potters)

ARMOIRE
Approximate size (in.): 72 x 36 x 20
Materials: maple, curly maple

BENCH
Approximate size (in.): 34 x 18 x 48
Materials: cherry, ash

CHINA CABINET
Approximate size (in.): 72 x 78 x 20
Materials: cherry, poplar, andaman padauk

P. O. Box 191
North Ferrisburg, VT 05473
(802) 877-2124
dhelms@together.net

DESIGN CHARGES:	$35 per hour rolled into purchase price
DEPOSIT:	25%–50% with balance due on completion
LEAD TIME:	2–6 months
LOCAL DELIVERY:	free within 50 miles
LONG DISTANCE:	best available shipper, plus crating charge

D. Andrew Kates, Cabinetmaker

"I believe in re-creating all aspects of a piece to retain its feel and integrity. I only use techniques and practices consistent with the period."

DON KATES believes that if you're reproducing a period original, you should work exactly as the maker of that original worked. Kates therefore uses only those wood species that were available to the original maker. He is also careful to use historically accurate tools and techniques, such as handplaning and scraping the surfaces of his work, assembling drawers using hand-cut dovetails, and applying finishes by hand. Kates even adjusts the condition of the finish so that it matches the look of the antique.

His work has appeared in juried shows in the Chicago area and in several publications, including *Early American Homes* and *Country Living*.

SHAKER SEWING DESK
Approximate size (in.): 40 x 31 x 24
Materials: cherry, bird's-eye maple

SOFA TABLE
Approximate size (in.): 30 x 60 x 16
Material: tiger maple

ENTERTAINMENT CENTER
Approximate size (in.): 76 x 42 x 25
Material: tiger maple

SHAKER TALL CLOCK
Approximate size (in.): 87 x 19 x 19
Material: cherry

702 Wingfoot Dr.
N. Aurora, IL 60542
(630) 482-3808
don@dandrewkates.com
www.dandrewkates.com

DESIGN CHARGES:	none when an order is placed
DEPOSIT:	40% with balance due on completion
LEAD TIME:	4–8 months
LOCAL DELIVERY:	$1 per mile, $50 minimum
LONG DISTANCE:	UPS or common carrier, plus crating charge up to 10% of price

Dan Mosheim Custom Furniture

"I think what attracts clients to my work is my willingness to listen, to try to form their words into sketches, drawings, models, and finally finished objects that reflect both their input and my own."

ALTHOUGH DAN MOSHEIM has developed a style loosely based on Biedermeier, Federal, and neoclassical elements, he is willing to design and produce furniture in many historical styles to suit the wishes of his clients. To that end, he uses whatever construction methods are appropriate for a particular piece. Mosheim is known for his designs that combine painted, stained, and natural woods. He has also developed a variety of inlays and appliqués that have become his hallmarks.

Mosheim's work has won awards at many regional shows. His work has also appeared on the pages of all seven of The Taunton Press' *Design Book* series, including the back cover of *Design Book Six.* In addition, his work has appeared in *Architectural Digest, Yankee, Vermont Magazine,* and *Country Living.*

DESK
Approximate size (in.): 30 x 60 x 30
Materials: mahogany, curly maple, walnut, rosewood, satinwood

POOL TABLE
Approximate size (in.): 60 x 110 x 32
Materials: figured cherry, slate

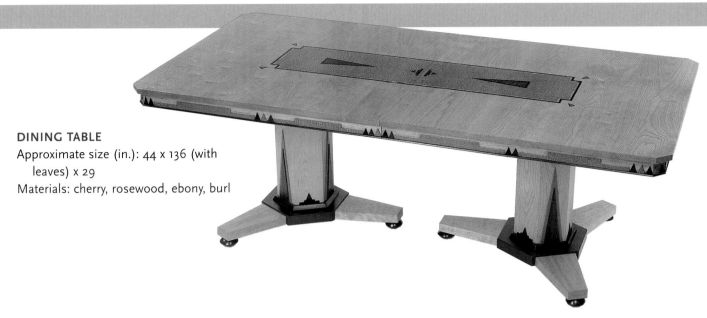

DINING TABLE
Approximate size (in.): 44 x 136 (with
  leaves) x 29
Materials: cherry, rosewood, ebony, burl

SIDEBOARD
Approximate size (in.): 34 x 72 x 20
Materials: cherry, rosewood, ebony, lacewood,
  red oak, pine

BUREAU
Approximate size (in.): 64 x 36 x 20
Materials: mahogany, walnut, curly maple, oak, pine

23 Goodwood Ln., P. O. Box 442
Dorset, VT 05251-0442
(802) 867-5541
FAX (802) 867-5541
dminc@vermontel.net
www.danmosheim.com

DESIGN CHARGES:	none
DEPOSIT:	10%–15%, with other payments made in stages and balance due on completion
LEAD TIME:	2½–3 months
LOCAL DELIVERY:	free
LONG DISTANCE:	blanket-wrap shipper

Darrell Peart, Furnituremaker

"I routinely work with clients to adapt the Arts and Crafts style (especially Greene and Greene) to a more contemporary setting or to suit their specific needs."

DARRELL PEART can identify many influences in the development of his design sensibility, ranging from Thomas Chippendale's 18th-century sense of proportion to James Krenov's 20th-century elegance, but Peart speaks (and designs) most passionately in the Greene and Greene vernacular. In fact, the designs of Greene and Greene possess an almost spiritual appeal for him.

Working mostly with solid woods, Peart uses a variety of traditional and contemporary construction methods. He assembles his casework using classical dovetail and mortise-and-tenon joinery, but when gluing up solid panels, he does make use of biscuits to align the components.

His work has appeared in *Today's Woodworker, Home Furniture,* and *Pacific Magazine.*

DETAIL

AUDIO CABINET ON STAND
Approximate size (in.): 49 x 22 x 18
Materials: cherry, wenge

DINING TABLE
Approximate size (in.): 30 x 53 x 94 (with leaves)
Materials: cherry, Ebon-X

ARMCHAIR
Approximate size (in.): 38 x 24 x 20
Materials: cherry, wenge, leather

SIDE CHAIR
Approximate size (in.): 38 x 18 x 18
Materials: cherry, wenge, leather

177 Western Ave. W.
Seattle, WA 98119
(425) 277-4070
FAX (425) 988-0117
darrell@furnituremaker.com
www.furnituremaker.com

DESIGN CHARGES:	$45 per hour
DEPOSIT:	20%, 20% 12 weeks prior to completion, with balance due on completion
LEAD TIME:	8–9 months
LOCAL DELIVERY:	free within 30 miles of Seattle
LONG DISTANCE:	best available shipper, plus crating charge

David Kiernan Furniture Designs

"What makes my business unique is me. My ability to understand a client's needs and my knowledge of design, materials, and techniques combine to provide a unique piece of furniture."

TEN YEARS AGO, David Kiernan was a dissatisfied and unfulfilled engineer until he visited an ACC craft show. Moved by the quality of the furniture displayed and tantalized by the craft schools advertising there, he decided to enroll in a two-year program at The Worcester Center for Crafts to embark on a second career as a furniture maker.

His original contemporary designs feature simplicity and elegance of form. Kiernan exhibits in many juried shows, including the Smithsonian Craft Show, the Philadelphia Museum of Art Craft Show, and the ACC Baltimore Show. His work has also appeared in *Design Book Seven* (The Taunton Press, 1996) and *American Craft* magazine.

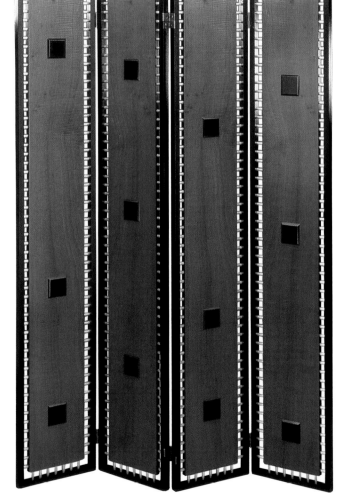

HALL TABLE
Approximate size (in.): 36 x 72 x 12
Materials: maple, mahogany, silver

SCREEN
Approximate size (in.): 72 x 48 x 1
Materials: curly makore, aluminum

WALL-HUNG CABINET

Approximate size (in.): 32 x 24 x 9
Materials: quilted mahogany, mahogany, ebony,
mirrored glass

DETAIL

DINING TABLE

Approximate size (in.): 29 x 60
Materials: lacewood, wenge,
aluminum

P. O. Box 248
Harmony, RI 02829
(401) 949-1548
FAX (401) 949-1548
dkiernan10@yahoo.com
www.davidkiernan.com

DESIGN CHARGES:	$45 per hour rolled into purchase price
DEPOSIT:	50% with balance due on completion
LEAD TIME:	4–6 months
LOCAL DELIVERY:	inquire
LONG DISTANCE:	best available shipper, plus crating charge (typically about 10% of purchase price)

David Sawyer, Windsor Chairs

"Every chair takes my best effort and attention to detail."

DAVE SAWYER sees Windsors as the Stradivari of chairs. In fact, his passionate belief in the perfection of this form made him hesitate before he began to build them because, in his words, "There's nowhere to go from there."

Sawyer identifies many reasons for his affection for this particular form, foremost being the Windsor's minimalist nature. As he points out, the chair is built without extras; there are no chrome bumpers or flashing lights. The only decoration appears in the turned or carved embellishments of the chair's structural components.

Another virtue of a well-made Windsor is its comfort, with its seat excavated to conform to the shape of the human bottom and the yielding spindles of its back. Finally, the Windsor appeals to Sawyer because, with the chair's extraordinary variety of forms, it offers the serious chairmaker a lifetime of challenges.

Sawyer's work can be found in homes all over the country as well as in the Museum of Fine Arts in Boston. It has also appeared in *Fine Woodworking* and *Home Furniture* magazines.

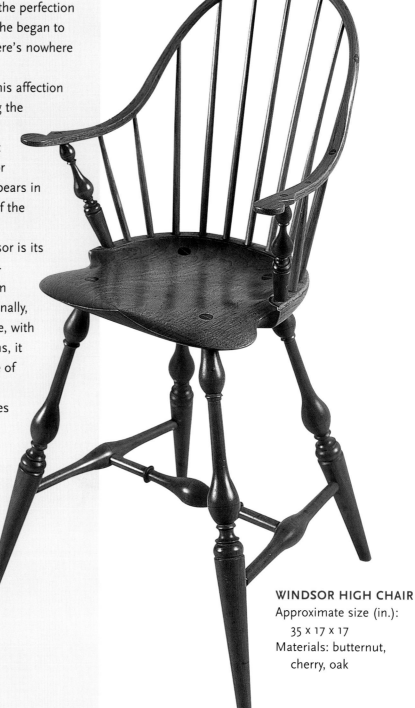

WINDSOR HIGH CHAIR
Approximate size (in.):
35 x 17 x 17
Materials: butternut,
cherry, oak

WINDSOR ROCKING-WRITING CHAIR
Approximate size (in.): 43 x 34 x 38
Materials: pine, maple, oak

WINDSOR TRIPLE SETTEE
Approximate size (in.): 38 x 69 x 20
Materials: butternut, cherry, oak

WINDSOR CONTINUOUS-ARM CHAIR
Approximate size (in.): 38 x 25 x 19
Materials: basswood, maple, oak

556 King Pond Rd.
East Calais, VT 05650
(802) 456-8836
(800) 968-2887
sawyer@bypass.com
www.windsorchairresources.com

DESIGN CHARGES:	none
DEPOSIT:	25% with balance due on completion
LEAD TIME:	8–12 months
LOCAL DELIVERY:	free
LONG DISTANCE:	best available shipper, plus crating charge

David Wright Windsors

"I choose to make one chair at a time, devoting my energy to seeing that each is expertly made."

DAVID WRIGHT builds his chairs the same way they were built by his 18th-century predecessors: one at a time and by hand. He begins by harvesting trees from the forested hills surrounding his Kentucky home, then continues by splitting the wood and transporting it to his shop, where it is rived into parts. He excavates seats with a gutter adze and inshave, turns his baluster legs on a lathe, and shaves spindles with a drawknife while holding them in place using his shaving horse. He then assembles and finishes the chair using traditional paints or natural oils. Throughout the process, Wright remains faithful to the long tradition of Windsor chairmaking.

His work has been exhibited in shows throughout Kentucky, Ohio, and Pennsylvania, winning best-of-show awards on several occasions. His work has also been featured on the pages of *Home Furniture*, *American Woodworker*, *American Woodturner*, and *Woodwork* magazines.

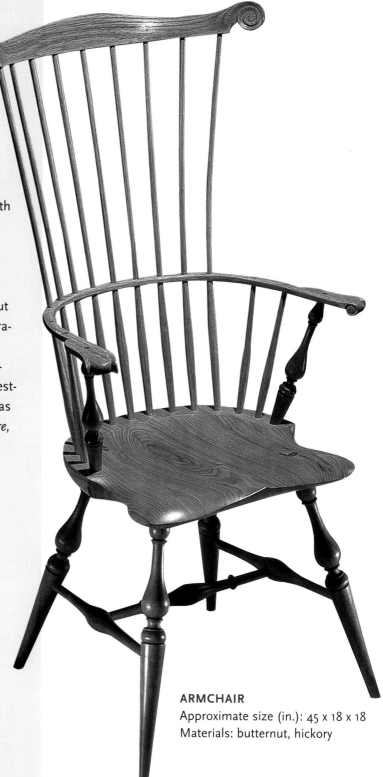

ARMCHAIR
Approximate size (in.): 45 x 18 x 18
Materials: butternut, hickory

ARMCHAIR
Approximate size (in.): 39 x 21 x 17
Materials: butternut, curly red oak

ARMCHAIR, TABLE
Approximate sizes (in.): 39 x 21 x 17 (chair), 25 x 15 (table)
Materials: cherry, oak (chair), cherry (table)

SIDE CHAIR
Approximate size (in.): 39 x 17 x 17
Materials: cherry, oak

P. O. Box 132
Berea, KY 40403
(859) 986-7962
wrightx4@earthlink.net

DESIGN CHARGES:	none
DEPOSIT:	25% with balance due on completion
LEAD TIME:	6–9 months
LOCAL DELIVERY:	free within 50 miles
LONG DISTANCE:	by freight or delivered by Wright for $0.65 per mile, plus crating charge of $75 per chair and $110 per settee

Design Sculpture in Wood

"We find great satisfaction in creating not only beautiful pieces of furniture but also good will with our clients."

EVERY PIECE that leaves the Vasquez shop is unique. This husband-and-wife team has no catalog of standard pieces; instead, working in many different styles, they create original designs that satisfy each client's needs.

Meeting clients' needs is, in fact, the guiding principle of their business, a principle not confined to the shop and the design studio. It extends also to the care they give to each client throughout the design and construction processes. This team believes commissioning original furniture should not be a stressful process for the client. It should be an exciting experience, one in which client and craftsman come together in the creation of something new and distinctive.

The work of the Vasquez shop has appeared in *San Diego Home and Garden Lifestyles* magazine, as well as in local newspapers.

TABLE AND CHAIRS
Approximate sizes (in.): 29 x 120 x 72 (table),
    52 x 20 x 18 (each chair)
Materials: ebony, sycamore, steel, glass, leather

TABLE AND CHAIRS
Approximate sizes (in.): 29 x 96 x 40 (table),
    38 x 20 x 18 (each chair)
Material: mahogany

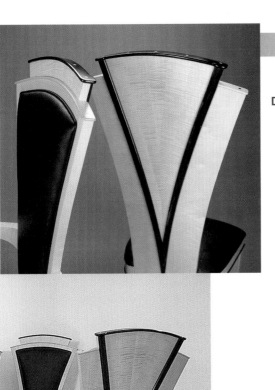

DETAIL

ENTERTAINMENT CENTER
Approximate size (in.): 78 x 120 x 30
Materials: figured English sycamore, makore

DETAIL

Ricardo and Joanne Vasquez
2215 30th St.
San Diego, CA 92104
(619) 283-3406
FAX (619) 283-3406
designsculpture@earthlink.net

DESIGN CHARGES:	inquire
DEPOSIT:	33%–50% with balance due on completion
LEAD TIME:	inquire
LOCAL DELIVERY:	inquire
LONG DISTANCE:	best available shipper, plus crating charge

Edmundson Fine Woodworking

"I see my work as creating balance through the careful choice of subtle details."

MARK EDMUNDSON believes that experiencing fine furniture is like experiencing gourmet food: "Too much spice will get your attention but won't necessarily please the palate." According to Edmundson, there are several ingredients that must be carefully measured and carefully mixed to produce a successful piece of furniture: quality materials, skillfully cut joinery, solid craftsmanship, and details that are unique to that piece. These qualities are evident in every piece that leaves his shop.

His work features both solid-wood and hand-cut veneers, all assembled using traditional joinery. He prefers shellac and oil finishes, although he does apply spray finishes if a customer requests it.

Edmundson has shown his furniture throughout the Northwest, including at the 1997 Chair Affair, where his work received the award for best design in the open category as well as the People's Choice award.

DRESSER
Approximate size (in.): 37 x 32 x 19
Materials: mahogany, maple, Spanish cedar

BENCH
Approximate size (in.): 27 x 42 x 16
Materials: cherry, Danish cord

DESK
Approximate size (in.): 30 x 41 x 20
Materials: olive ash, curly maple,
  rosewood

FLOOR CABINET
Approximate size (in.): 35 x 16 x 12
Materials: cherry, kwila, Spanish
  cedar

Mark Edmundson
1965 Samuels Rd.
Sandpoint, ID 83864
(208) 265-8730, (866) 877-1882
FAX (208) 265-8730
mark@efinewoodworking.com
www.efinewoodworking.com

DESIGN CHARGES: none
DEPOSIT: 50% with balance due
                   on completion
LEAD TIME: 1½–2 months
LOCAL DELIVERY: free
LONG DISTANCE: best available shipper,
                   plus crating charge

18th–Century New England Fine Country Furniture

"My early work was done exclusively with hand tools. In the interest of time, I sought training and apprenticed using machinery, but I still insist on using hand tools to augment and distinguish my work."

GEOFFREY AMES entered the woodworking field through the back door, beginning as an antiques collector who was forced to build furniture because he couldn't afford to buy the originals he really wanted. Ames specializes in reproductions of New England country furniture of the 17th and 18th centuries. But unlike many who reproduce such furniture, Ames completes each piece by applying a finish he calls "as found." An "as found" finish replicates the appearance of 200-year-old furniture. He achieves this appearance by using layer upon layer of paint, varnish, and lacquer.

Ames's work has appeared in juried exhibitions throughout New Hampshire. His five-drawer Queen Anne chest-on-frame appears on the dust jacket of Dean Fales's book *American Painted Furniture 1660–1880*, as well as on the cover of *Objects of Desire*.

PAINTED AND GRAINED SECRETARY
Approximate size (in.): 82 x 33 x 20
Material: pine

SPANISH-FOOT RAM'S-HORN ARM CHAIR
Approximate size (in.): 44 x 25 x 26
Material: maple

BUTTERFLY TABLE WITH SPLAYED DRAWER
Approximate size (in.): 28 x 42 x 35
Material: curly maple

BOSTON QUEEN ANNE SIDE CHAIR
Approximate size (in.): 41 x 23 x 22
Material: mahogany

Geoffrey Ames
HC 74, Box 10b, Rte. 126
Center Strafford, NH 03815
(603) 269-3571
newt@worldpath.net

DESIGN CHARGES:	$60 per hour rolled into purchase price
DEPOSIT:	50% with balance due on completion
LEAD TIME:	2–3 months
LOCAL DELIVERY:	$0.35 per mile (round trip) plus $25
LONG DISTANCE:	inquire

Eric Englander Cabinet and Furniture Making

"The clients have to place themselves in another era where the time taken to accomplish a piece of furniture was equal to the quality of the piece they receive in the end."

ERIC ENGLANDER places no limits on the kinds of woodworking assignments he will accept. He is as comfortable building a Biedermeier-style cabinet as he is building a Chippendale-style side chair. This versatility, he believes, is what sets him apart. His clients have the unique opportunity of having one source to fulfill all their furniture and architectural woodworking needs.

In his previous career, Englander was a theatrical carpenter, building scenery for Broadway plays, films, and television productions. Then, wishing to build more enduring work, he attended the North Bennet Street School in Boston, where he acquired the technical skills required by his new career as a furniture maker.

He has exhibited in several New York and New England venues. His work was awarded first prize in the 1999 and 2000 annual "A Celebration of the Individual Craftsman" shows put on by the Mystic Art Association.

BIEDERMEIER TELEVISION CABINET
Approximate size (in.): 74 x 40 x 22
Materials: basswood, walnut

BIEDERMEIER WALNUT SIDE CHAIRS
Approximate size (in.): 39 x 18 x 18 (each)
Materials: walnut, upholstery

CARVED OAK TRESTLE TABLE
Approximate size (in.): 29 x 36 x 72
Materials: red oak, walnut,
 Spanish tiles

9 Olive Sq.
Somerville, MA 02143
(617) 623-5150
FAX (617) 623-4657
eengla@mediaone.net
www.ericenglander.com

DESIGN CHARGES:	15% of projected price rolled into purchase price
DEPOSIT:	50% with balance due on completion
LEAD TIME:	4–6 months
LOCAL DELIVERY:	$150
LONG DISTANCE:	common carrier, plus crating charge

Fogelvik Furniture

"A high level of integrity, clear communications, and excellent customer relations are very important to me."

MATS FOGELVIK wants to elicit the "wow" effect. He wants to create furniture that irresistibly compels the viewer to reach out and touch its surfaces, which—although they may appear to ripple—are smooth to the touch.

In part, he achieves the "wow" effect through the use of curly koa, a figured variety of a wood unique to Hawaii. As important, however, is Fogelvik's marriage of this visually arresting species to designs he describes as balanced and peaceful.

Fogelvik began his training in a one-year program at Nyckelvikskolan in Stockholm, Sweden. His Swedish background is evident in his Arts and Crafts-inspired designs. His work has won recognition at a number of shows in Hawaii. He currently exhibits at the Arthur Dennis Williams Gallery in Maui.

HALL TABLE
Approximate size (in.): 32 x 24 x 17
Materials: curly koa, tamarind, rosewood

DETAIL

DETAIL

DINING TABLE
Approximate size (in.): 30 x 40 x 73
Materials: curly koa, wenge

CHAIR
Approximate size (in.): 34 x 17 x 18
Materials: curly koa, wenge

Mats Fogelvik
P. O. Box 826
Makawao, HI 96768
(808) 575-7678
FAX (808) 572-3440
furniture@fogelvik.com
www.fogelvik.com

DESIGN CHARGES:	only for extensive effort with any cost rolled into purchase price
DEPOSIT:	50% with balance due on completion
LEAD TIME:	3 months
LOCAL DELIVERY:	free on the island of Maui
LONG DISTANCE:	air freight, plus $50–$300 crating charge

John Reed Fox

"Use a particular artist because you love his voice. Then let him be creative."

JOHN REED FOX, a self-taught craftsman, has been building furniture for 21 years. Although he identifies his work as "studio furniture," functionality is an important element in his approach to design. Even more important is the idea that through his or her work, each maker speaks in a unique voice. Fox says, "My goal is simply to find my own voice in the process of creating furniture that is functional, decorative, and elegant."

He assembles his furniture from solid wood using traditional joinery. Then he creates the final surfaces without using abrasives, relying instead on handplanes and spokeshaves.

His work has been featured in a number of national magazines, including *Fine Woodworking, Home Furniture,* and *Woodwork.* In addition, his work has appeared in galleries and shows throughout the United States.

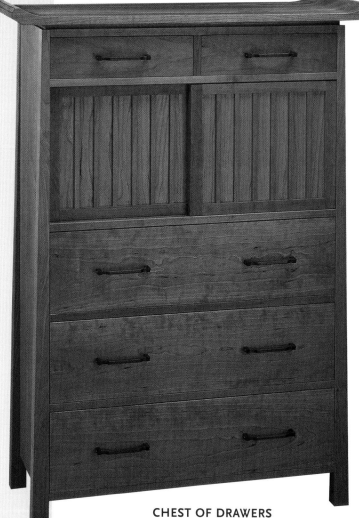

CHEST OF DRAWERS
Approximate size (in.): 50 x 38 x 17
Materials: cherry, pau ferro, maple, basswood

SIDEBOARD
Approximate size (in.): 32 x 63 x 17
Materials: walnut, maple

SILVERWARE CABINET
Approximate size (in.): 32 x 32 x 17
Materials: cherry, rosewood, maple

COLLECTOR'S CABINET
Approximate size (in.): 54 x 29 x 15
Materials: cherry, rosewood

DETAIL

179 Pope Rd.
Acton, MA 01720
(978) 635-0807

DESIGN CHARGES:	$350 per piece rolled into purchase price
DEPOSIT:	amount depends on total price
LEAD TIME:	8–16 months
LOCAL DELIVERY:	free
LONG DISTANCE:	blanket-wrap art carrier

Fox Brothers

"In our exploration of nontraditional design elements and materials, we have conceived of our furniture as an alignment of light, tension, weight, and the unexpected. Our individuality emerges from a foundation of wood accented with the innovative use of unusual materials."

HENRY FOX sees the furniture produced in the Fox Brothers' shop as a physical manifestation of the voices of the furniture makers who designed and built it. "This is our voice, spoken through our hands," he explains. "It is a passionate pursuit of that which is thought provoking and out of the ordinary."

The Fox Brothers' shop prides itself on having the flexibility to produce a single piece of furniture or, when a client requests it, an entire houseful of furniture. One recent commission required them to build 80 pieces for a single home.

The work of the Fox Brothers has appeared in many exhibits on the East Coast, including at the Smithsonian Craft Show the last three years.

ZERO CHAIR
Approximate size (in.): 56 x 23 x 20
Materials: cherry, ash, dacron

SIDEBOARD
Approximate size (in.): 32 x 79 x 22
Materials: anigre, bronze, ebony

O2 CHAIR
Approximate size (in.): 42 x 20 x 22
Materials: tiger maple, stainless
steel

ABRACADABRA SIDEBOARD
Approximate size (in.): 32 x 68 x 20
Materials: cherry, bird's-eye maple,
copper roofing

Henry Fox
39 Liberty St.
Newburyport, MA 01950
(978) 462-7726
FAX (978) 462-7717
hsfox@earthlink.net

DESIGN CHARGES:	$300 rolled into purchase price
DEPOSIT:	50% with balance due on completion
LEAD TIME:	6–18 months
LOCAL DELIVERY:	inquire
LONG DISTANCE:	best available shipper, plus crating charge

Gallery Woodworking Company

"The Japanese approach to woodworking has become integral in my design and execution processes."

TOM OWENS'S brief experience training with a Japanese temple carpenter in Northern California has had a lasting influence on his work as a furniture maker, an influence that has manifested itself in two very different ways. During that training, Owens was allowed to purchase a chisel only after several days of work. He was then not permitted to apply that chisel to wood until he had completed several weeks of daily sharpening sessions and until his mind had been emptied of distractions through hard labor.

This focused instruction gave Owens a keen appreciation of the value of properly maintained and properly employed hand tools. In addition, although he describes his current work as Craftsman inspired, there are, nevertheless, many qualities in that work that evoke traditional Japanese and Chinese furniture, in particular, the attention Owens gives to a careful balancing of mass and color. Working with two partners, Owens creates his furniture on a commission-only basis, using solid wood, traditional hand-cut joinery, and handplanes to create his final surfaces.

DETAIL

COFFEE TABLE
Approximate size (in.): 18 x 40 x 20
Materials: wenge, white oak, mahogany, bamboo

DETAIL

ARMOIRE
Approximate size (in.): 58 x 40 x 22
Materials: oak, wenge, mahogany,
curly cherry, Peruvian walnut

DINING TABLE
Approximate size (in.): 30 x 38 x 72
(with extensions)
Materials: oak, mahogany, walnut,
copper

Tom Owens
593-2 George Wilson Rd.
Boone, NC 28607
(828) 264-8971
FAX (828) 264-8971
handmade@boone.net
www.gallerywoodworking.com

DESIGN CHARGES:	inquire
DEPOSIT:	25% with balance due on completion
LEAD TIME:	3 months
LOCAL DELIVERY:	inquire
LONG DISTANCE:	air freight, plus crating charge

83

John Gallis

"We design western furniture that is never machined so much you forget the wood was once a tree."

JOHN GALLIS designs and builds furniture in which the connection between tree and finished object is boldly written in the rough muscularity of debarked but often unsawn material. Using 200-year-old walnut slabs trimmed with juniper, Gallis and his four employees produce a line of home furnishings that evoke the spirit of the western state in which they are created.

Gallis has been in business for 27 years, beginning in New York, then moving to Wyoming in 1995. The move was apparently successful: In the years following the move, Gallis's work won Exhibitor's Choice (1997), People's Choice (1998), and Best Craftsmanship (1999) awards at the Western Design Conference, as well as the 2000 Switchback Ranch Purchase Award.

DETAIL

SLAB DESK
Approximate size (in.): 31 x 80 x 51
Materials: spalted maple, juniper, walnut

BED
Approximate sizes (in.): 64 x 82 (headboard), 38 x 82 (footboard)
Material: walnut

LOVE SEAT
Approximate size (in.): 39 x 51 x 24
Material: walnut

38 Rd. 2 AB
Cody, WY 82414
(307) 587-7777
www.norsemandesignswest.com

DESIGN CHARGES:	none
DEPOSIT:	50% with balance due on completion
LEAD TIME:	3–4 months
LOCAL DELIVERY:	free
LONG DISTANCE:	inquire

Gloor Design

"My designs are a fusion of masculine and feminine—powerful, with simple grace and elegant strength."

MICHAEL GLOOR describes his work as "neo-Shaker meets the Orient." That comment may inspire some head scratching, but it does suggest the many influences—from Shaker to Art Deco—that Gloor seeks to synthesize in his work.

He matches his working processes to the requirements of each piece, using veneers, as he explains, "for their showiness and stability and solid wood for its grace and structural strength." He then applies clear, nontoxic finishes to allow the wood to speak for itself.

His work has appeared in *Home Furniture Monthly* magazine, as well as in *Rhode Island Monthly* and other regional publications. In addition, he was featured on an episode of HGTV's *Modern Masters* series, which aired in January 2000.

LUNA SERIES PEDESTAL TABLE
Approximate size (in.): 29 x 42
Materials: satinwood, mahogany

CURVED-FRONT BUREAU
Approximate size (in.): 44 x 32 x 20
Materials: bird's-eye elm, bubinga,
purpleheart

**TEMPLE SERIES
CHINA CABINET**
Approximate size (in.):
58 x 64 x 24
Materials: quilted maple,
mahogany, ebony

PAGODA SERIES COFFEE TABLE
Approximate size (in.): 22 x 50 x 18
Materials: sycamore, mahogany, koa

Michael Gloor
51 Green St.
Peace Dale, RI 02883
(401) 782-2443
FAX (401) 782-2443
mgloor@gloordesign.com
www.gloordesign.com

DESIGN CHARGES:	none
DEPOSIT:	50% with balance due on completion
LEAD TIME:	2–3 months
LOCAL DELIVERY:	inquire
LONG DISTANCE:	UPS or freight, plus crating charge

Jeffrey P. Greene

"American furniture of the 18th century had an unmatched spirit of design and integrity of craftsmanship, and the Newport cabinetmakers developed a unique style that integrated ornament with excellent proportions."

JEFFREY P. GREENE builds furniture that is both beautiful and historically accurate. He specializes in replicating the furniture of the Goddard and Townsend families of cabinetmakers who worked in 18th-century Newport, Rhode Island. This focus results in furniture Greene describes as "a blend of history, design, and craftsmanship that is recognized by serious collectors."

Greene builds each piece individually, using hand-cut mortise-and-tenon and dovetail joinery and adding, where the historical antecedent requires it, hand-carved decorative elements. He then creates the final surfaces using handplanes and hand scrapers.

His work has appeared on the pages of *Fine Furniture International, Traditional Home, Early American Life, Architectural Digest,* and *Fine Woodworking.* He is also the author of *American Furniture of the 18th Century: History, Technique, Structure* (The Taunton Press, 1996). In addition, Greene is licensed by several museums to replicate for sale the furniture displayed in their collections.

BONNET-TOP NEWPORT HIGH CHEST
Approximate size (in.): 87 x 42 x 23
Material: mahogany

MARBLE-TOP SIDE TABLE
Approximate size (in.): 28 x 46 x 23
Materials: mahogany, marble

KNEEHOLE BUREAU
Approximate size (in.): 35 x 36 x 21
Material: mahogany

CORNER CHAIR
Approximate size (in.): 31 x 17 x 17
Material: mahogany

55 America's Cup Ave.
Newport, RI 02840
(401) 848-5600
FAX (401) 848-5650
www.theballandclaw.com

DESIGN CHARGES:	none
DEPOSIT:	50% with balance due on completion
LEAD TIME:	24 months
LOCAL DELIVERY:	inquire
LONG DISTANCE:	blanket-wrap delivery or crated air freight

Gregg Lipton Furniture

"I like to reach a place in my work where nothing need be added or taken away. The result should be a refined, timeless, and original piece that peels away the distractions and speaks to the fundamental form."

GREGG LIPTON is consciously committed to the process of innovation. He wants each piece of furniture that leaves his shop to represent a unique solution to the age-old design problems: where to sit, to eat, to work, to relax, to sleep, and to store.

Although this self-taught woodworker prefers the strength of such traditional woodworking mainstays as the mortise-and-tenon joint, he also strives to use modern shop practices. He has, for example, embraced the use of certain veneers, which were not available to his 18th- and 19th-century predecessors.

Lipton's work has earned him recognition in many venues, including dozens of articles in books, magazines, and newspapers. He has also shown his work in exhibitions and museums across the country, including in the Smithsonian Craft Show the last two years.

DESK
Approximate size (in.): 30 x 48 x 24
Material: padauk

SIDEBOARD
Approximate size (in.): 32 x 50 x 20
Materials: quilted maple, maple, ebony, glass

GAZELLE SIDEBOARD
Approximate size (in.): 34 x 60 x 21
Materials: cherry, stainless steel

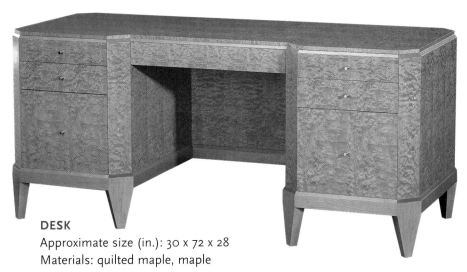

DESK
Approximate size (in.): 30 x 72 x 28
Materials: quilted maple, maple

1 Mill Ridge Rd.
Cumberland, ME 04021
(207) 829-5010
FAX (207) 829-3128
gregg@liptonfurniture.com
www.liptonfurniture.com

DESIGN CHARGES: $500 rolled into
purchase price

DEPOSIT: 50% with balance due
on completion

LEAD TIME: 7–9 months

LOCAL DELIVERY: inquire

LONG DISTANCE: blanket-wrap shipper,
plus crating charge

Gregory W. Guenther, Furniture Maker

"We are a seasoned group of furniture makers dedicated to creating fine, lasting furniture with an emphasis on hand-worked surfaces and joinery."

TWENTY YEARS OF EXPERIENCE in both the restoration of antique furniture and in the creation of new furniture has equipped Greg Guenther with the necessary skills and the aesthetic judgment to tackle virtually any fine-furniture commission that comes his way. His shop skills include veneering, carving, turning, finishing, and, of course, hand-cut joinery. The styles in which he works are similarly extensive, ranging from the sleek modernism of the music stand shown on the facing page to the Chippendale/Gothic breakfront shown at right.

His work has appeared in many national woodworking magazines, and he has been featured on two network television shows, *The New Yankee Workshop* and HGTV's *Modern Masters*.

DETAIL

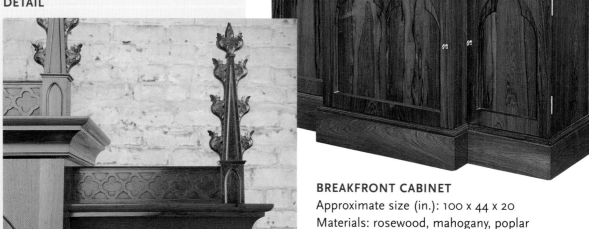

BREAKFRONT CABINET
Approximate size (in.): 100 x 44 x 20
Materials: rosewood, mahogany, poplar

MUSIC STAND
Approximate size (in.): 48 x 16 x 16
Materials: mahogany, bubinga, poplar

CHIPPENDALE-STYLE BED
Approximate size (in.): 110 x 68 x 88
Materials: walnut, yellow pine

409 E. York St.
Savannah, GA 31401
(912) 447-5522
FAX (912) 447-5522

DESIGN CHARGES:	inquire
DEPOSIT:	50% followed by 25% halfway through construction with the final 25% due on completion
LEAD TIME:	3–6 months
LOCAL DELIVERY:	FOB
LONG DISTANCE:	specialty carriers, plus crating charge

Grew–Sheridan Studio

"I'm drawn to solo woodworking and the life of a craftsman because it holds the promise of being a satisfying, nonexploitative, creative, and ever-stimulating endeavor that suits my eyes and hands."

TWENTY-FIVE YEARS AGO, John Sheridan entered the woodworking field with his late wife Carolyn. Together they built careers that brought them national recognition not only as craftspeople but also as teachers in the woodworking field.

Now in his wife's absence, Sheridan carries on the tradition of building furniture he describes as "classic contemporary with Modernist overtones." The furniture has simple curves and tightly controlled angles and presents "austere forms in a world of visual complexity." In addition, he continues to teach classes out of his San Francisco shop and is creating a furniture program at the Academy of Art College.

Sheridan's work has appeared in many shows around the country. He is also the author of dozens of articles in woodworking magazines.

CHAIR
Approximate size (in.): 46 x 45 x 34
Materials: maple, plywood

ALTAR
Approximate size (in.): 37 x 72 x 21
Material: white oak

"LUNAR" DINING TABLE
Approximate size (in.): 29 x 60
Materials: glass, copper, rubber, maple

COUNTER STOOL
Approximate size (in.): 29 x 18 x 12
Materials: walnut, ash

John Sheridan
3450 Third St., 5E
San Francisco, CA 94124
(415) 824-6161
FAX (415) 970-9626

DESIGN CHARGES:	$41 per hour, not rolled into purchase price
DEPOSIT:	33%, successive payments spread out over construction process
LEAD TIME:	4 months
LOCAL DELIVERY:	$41 per hour, plus $20 per hour for assistant
LONG DISTANCE:	air freight, plus crating charge

GWC Design

"Most of my work is based on clean, classical lines with a contemporary edge."

GIFFORD COCHRAN has a degree in environmental design and architecture from the University of Colorado at Boulder. The balanced, symmetrical, and geometric work he now produces reflects his years of architectural study in addition to his desire to create furniture attuned to the personality of each client.

Cochran works with solid hardwood, primarily figured maple, cherry, and walnut, accenting these species with various kinds of inlaid material. He employs traditional joinery and applies either lacquer or hand-rubbed oil and wax finishes.

His work has been exhibited at the Danforth Gallery in Livingston, Montana, and at the Artifacts Gallery in Bozeman, Montana. He received the Best of Show Table Category award at the Los Angeles Design Show in 1999.

DETAIL

SIDEBOARD
Approximate size (in.): 36 x 72 x 24
Materials: figured walnut, walnut burl, ebony

WRITING DESK AND CHAIR

Approximate sizes (in.): 30 x 58 x 30 (desk), 42 x 20 x 20 (chair)
Materials: figured cherry, walnut burl, bird's-eye maple, leather

DETAIL

Gifford W. Cochran
4850 River Rd.
Bozeman, MT 59718
(406) 388-7490
(406) 388-8120
gwc@avicom.net
www.gwcdesign.com

DESIGN CHARGES:	$20 per hour rolled into purchase price
DEPOSIT:	50% with balance due on completion
LEAD TIME:	1½ months
LOCAL DELIVERY:	free
LONG DISTANCE:	best available shipper, plus crating charge

Heitzman Studios

"I have always felt furniture should do more than simply serve a practical purpose; it should also offer a unique visual expression that enhances yet transcends function."

ROGER HEITZMAN is a modernist, not only in terms of the finished work he produces but also in his approach to the creation of that work. Although he does sketch manually during the design process, he will also switch to a computer-aided design (CAD) system to help himself and his client visualize all three dimensions of a planned piece of furniture.

Regardless of his method, what Heitzman is seeking—both in the design studio and in the shop—is that moment of harmony when the dictates of design, function, and construction all come together.

Heitzman's work has appeared in exhibitions throughout California. It has also been featured in many national woodworking publications.

NOUVEAU BUFFET
Approximate size (in.): 84 x 87 x 32
Materials: mahogany, granite, glass, bronze

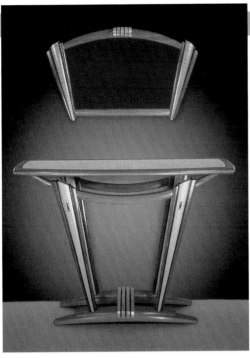

HALL TABLE AND MIRROR
Approximate size (in.): 36 x 45 x 11 (table)
Materials: mahogany, fiddleback anigre, bubinga,
    maple, wenge, mirrored glass

DECO CREDENZA
Approximate size (in.): 32 x 50 x 22
Materials: 12 species

DECO CABINET
Approximate size (in.): 50 x 23 x 15
Materials: mahogany, wenge,
    anigre, 11 additional species

Roger Heitzman
750 Whispering Pines
Scotts Valley, CA 95066
(831) 438-1118
FAX (831) 438-4043
heitzman@scruznet.com
www.heitzmanstudios.com

DESIGN CHARGES:	$50 per hour rolled into purchase price
DEPOSIT:	30% with balance due at completion
LEAD TIME:	3–6 months
LOCAL DELIVERY:	usually included in price
LONG DISTANCE:	blanket-wrap shipper, plus crating charge

Heritage Woodcraft, Inc., Design Studio, Fine Woodworking

"All that we have—the wood, the ideas, the abilities—are a heritage that has been handed down. Our goal is to be good stewards."

JIM ZOLLINGER strives to be a good steward of the woodworking heritage with which he and all contemporary woodworkers have been gifted. In addition to using butterfly joints, he employs mortise-and-tenon and dovetail joinery, and many of his finishes are of hand-rubbed oil. But Zollinger is not willing to turn his back on the present. His shop is equipped to apply spray finishes, and he has begun producing furniture featuring slab material.

Zollinger prizes opportunities to collaborate with artists from other disciplines, recently teaming with an architect/builder in the production of architectural woodwork. In fact, Zollinger believes his experience collaborating with other artists is one of the qualities that distinguishes his company's work.

LAMP STAND
Approximate size (in.):
22 x 17 x 17
Material: walnut

COFFEE TABLE
Approximate size (in.): 16 x 51 x 18
Materials: lacewood, bubinga

SOFA TABLE
Approximate size (in.): 33 x 48 x 17
Materials: walnut, ash

CORNER DISPLAY SHELF
Approximate size (in.): 63 x 12 x 12
Material: figured maple

Jim Zollinger
1871 Hibbard Rd. NE
Silverton, OR 97381
(503) 873-4789
FAX (503) 873-4789
www.heritagewoodcraft.com

DESIGN CHARGES:	$45 per hour rolled into purchase price
DEPOSIT:	33% with balance due on completion
LEAD TIME:	3–6 months
LOCAL DELIVERY:	free
LONG DISTANCE:	Fed Ex, or common carrier, plus crating charge

Ian Ingersoll Cabinetmakers

"To Shakerize a design has become the basis of my own work as I strive to create modern designs that have their origins in the past but the look of the future."

TWENTY-FIVE YEARS AGO, Ian Ingersoll began his career as a furniture maker by copying Shaker originals. He chose this approach for two reasons. First, he saw it as a way to apprentice himself to a master's work. Although he couldn't stand behind those 19th-century Shaker craftsmen and watch them work, the story of their shop practices was written in the furniture they left behind. The second, more obvious reason for Ingersoll's choice is that this work was available in his native New England. Since that time, he has worked in many other styles but always under the influence of his early study of Shaker work.

His work has appeared in many magazines, including *Metropolitan Home, House Beautiful, Early American Life,* and on the cover of *Home Furniture.* In addition, his work has been in many national and international exhibitions.

#7 MT. LEBANON ROCKING CHAIR
Approximate size (in.): 43 x 25 x 31
Materials: cherry, Shaker tape

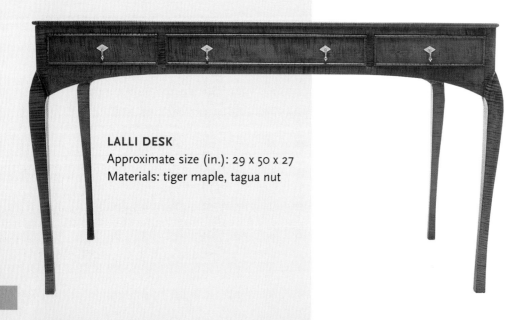

LALLI DESK
Approximate size (in.): 29 x 50 x 27
Materials: tiger maple, tagua nut

12 DRAWER CHEST
Approximate size (in.): 88 x 36 x 17
Materials: bird's-eye maple, cherry

WILLIAM AND MARY CHEST
Approximate size (in.): 52 x 32 x 13
Materials: tiger maple, tagua nut

1 Main St.
West Cornwall, CT 06796
(860) 672-6334
FAX (860) 672-0355
ian@ianingersoll.com
www.ianingersoll.com

DESIGN CHARGES:	none
DEPOSIT:	50% with balance due on completion
LEAD TIME:	1½–2 months
LOCAL DELIVERY:	4% of purchase price
LONG DISTANCE:	common carrier or blanket-wrap shipper, plus crating charge

Irion Company Furniture Makers

"Our approach to making furniture is from the perspective of the 18th century, and we work hard to capture that spirit in every piece of furniture we make."

THE CABINETMAKERS who work in the Irion Company shop strive to make their work like that produced by their 18th-century predecessors. This process begins with the careful selection of wide and matched lumber, giving places of honor to those boards exhibiting striking grain, color, and figure.

Unlike some in the reproduction business who seek to minimize the amount of handwork required, the cabinetmakers in the Irion Company have looked for opportunities to introduce more handwork into their shop routine. All surfaces are handplaned and hand-scraped, all dovetails are cut by hand, and all the carving is done by hand. This produces furniture with a texture no machine methods can mimic. In addition, the Irion Company requires that a single craftsman build each piece from start to finish, adding his signature to the completed work.

The furniture of the Irion Company has appeared in many national and regional magazines, including *Fine Woodworking* and *Home Furniture*.

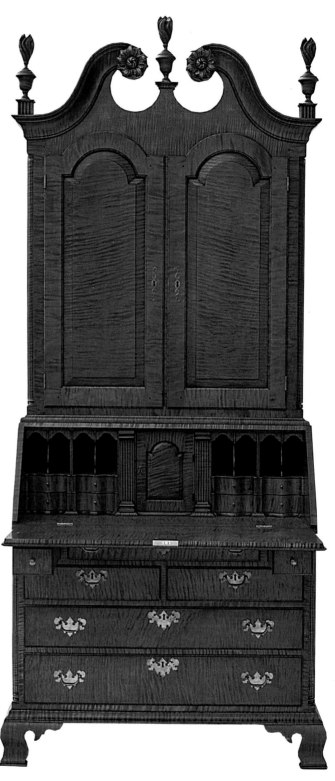

PHILADELPHIA SECRETARY
Approximate size (in.): 96 x 38 x 22
Material: crotch walnut

DUNLAP HIGH CHEST
Approximate size (in.): 84 x 38 x 21
Material: tiger maple

LANCASTER COUNTY
HIGH CHEST
Approximate size (in.):
95 x 42 x 22
Material: crotch walnut

DETAIL

Kendl Monn
1 South Bridge St.
Christiana, PA 17509
(610) 593-2153
(610) 593-2651

DESIGN CHARGES:	inquire
DEPOSIT:	10%–50% with balance due on completion
LEAD TIME:	3–24 months
LOCAL DELIVERY:	free
LONG DISTANCE:	best available shipper, plus crating charge

Jacobs Reproductions

"I believe if a piece is built well, it should pass the test of time to become an antique of the future. This is the vision I have for my work."

DURING HIS STUDY at Rockingham Community College, Jamie Becker developed a healthy respect for the enduring quality of the 18th-century furniture he observed there. Today with the help of three employees, Becker focuses on furniture that either reproduces or is inspired by specific 18th-century originals. The pieces range from Windsor chairs to high-style Goddard-and-Townsend casework. All are built using the same techniques as those employed by Becker's predecessors.

Becker's work has appeared in a number of exhibitions in the St. Louis area, and for the last three years he has been listed as one of the Top 200 Craftsmen in America by *Early American Homes* magazine. He was also selected by the White House to create a piece of furniture that is now a part of its permanent collection.

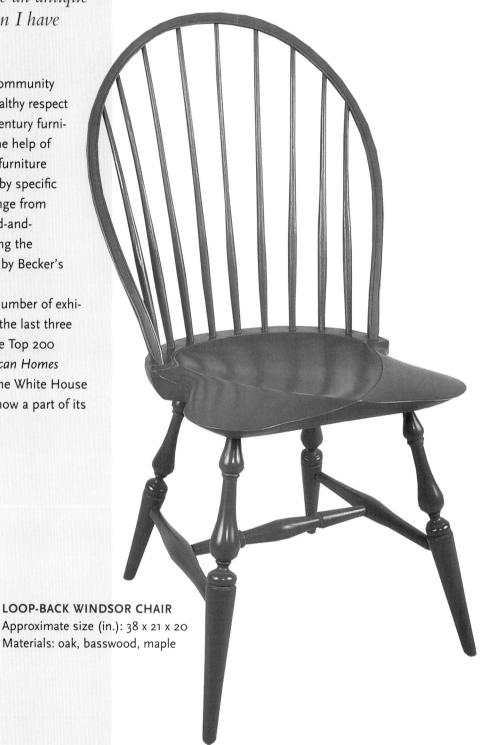

LOOP-BACK WINDSOR CHAIR
Approximate size (in.): 38 x 21 x 20
Materials: oak, basswood, maple

BLANKET CHEST
Approximate size (in.): 15 x 32 x 13
Material: curly cherry

DEMILUNE TABLE
Approximate size (in.): 29 x 36 x 20
Materials: anigre, laurel, walnut, maple

NEWPORT BLOCK-FRONT CHEST
Approximate size (in.): 33 x 37 x 23
Material: mahogany

Jamie Becker
2819 W. Delmar
Godfrey, IL 62035
(618) 466-5307
www.jacobsreproductions.com

DESIGN CHARGES:	none
DEPOSIT:	50% with balance due on completion
LEAD TIME:	4 months
LOCAL DELIVERY:	$40 per hour
LONG DISTANCE:	UPS, or common carrier, plus crating charge

Jamie Robertson Designs

"Each of my furniture pieces is an art object. They each redefine the distinction between the exclusive domains of function and aesthetics."

WHEN JAMIE ROBERTSON talks about his work, he talks about two things: artistry and craftsmanship. In the realm of artistry, he discusses color schemes, patterns, trompe l'oeil effects, and skewed rules of perspective. In the realm of craftsmanship, he refers to handles designed to fit human fingers, to doors that open accompanied by a soft exhalation of air from the closed cabinet, to drawers that glide open or closed in response to a gentle push. These are the hallmarks of his work.

Robertson's work has been exhibited in galleries across the United States. His work has also appeared on the pages of dozens of magazines and newspapers, including The Taunton Press' *Design Book* series, *American Woodworker,* the *Boston Globe,* and *New York* magazine.

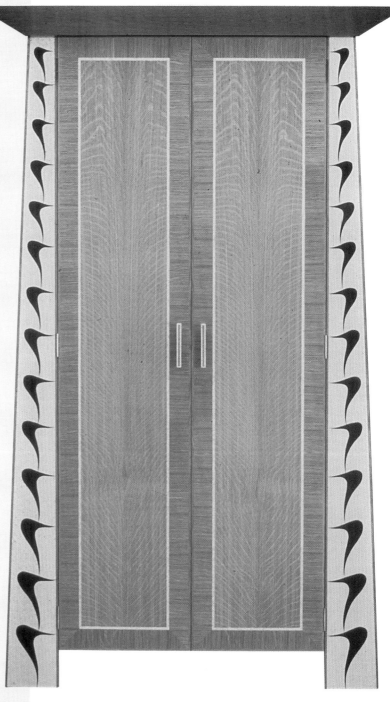

ARMOIRE
Approximate size (in.): 75 x 47 x 31
Materials: bird's-eye maple, white oak, plywood

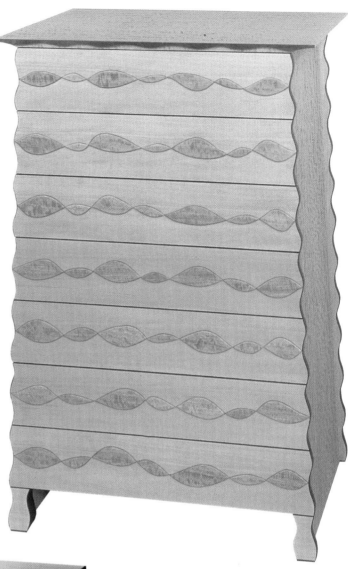

CHEST OF DRAWERS
Approximate size (in.): 48 x 33 x 22
Materials: satinwood, purpleheart,
poplar, mahogany, cherry, plywood

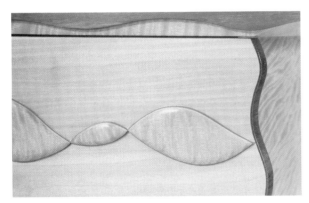

DETAIL

BEDSIDE TABLES
Approximate size (in.): 26 x 20 x 18 (each)
Materials: lemonwood, pau amarello, rosewood

43 Bradford St.
Concord, MA 01742
(978) 371-1106
FAX (978) 371-1809

DESIGN CHARGES:	$50 per hour rolled into purchase price
DEPOSIT:	33% with second payment midway through construction and balance due on completion
LEAD TIME:	3 months
LOCAL DELIVERY:	inquire
LONG DISTANCE:	best available shipper, plus crating charge of $200–$400

Seth Janofsky

"Good design results more often from the dedicated search for the best possible fulfillment of the competing demands of form, function, and value than from fanaticism, fetishism, or the search for 'originality' or 'self-expression.'"

ALTHOUGH HE DOES NOT MAKE "Japanese" furniture, seeing it rather as a synthesis of European modern and other sensibilities, Seth Janofsky recognizes that his work has been profoundly influenced by Japanese culture. In broad terms, this influence is simply an acknowledgment of the intimate way handmade objects are integrated into a traditional Japanese lifestyle.

But Janofsky also sees reflections of Japanese aesthetics in his own personal design vision, a design vision that leads him to strive for what he identifies as the serenity of traditional Japanese design and architecture. Recently he has begun to deliberately introduce to his furniture various Japanese motifs, specifically the abstraction of natural motifs into patterns.

Janofsky's work has been widely exhibited in California. It has also appeared in *Fine Woodworking, American Woodworker, Home Furniture,* and *Woodwork* magazines.

CABINET
Approximate size (in.): 44 x 38 x 15
Materials: white oak, maple, various woods

TALL DISPLAY CABINET

Approximate size (in.): 60 x 43 x 21
Materials: cherry, red oak, pine

HUMIDOR

Approximate size (in.): 6 x 15 x 11
Materials: walnut, Spanish cedar, white oak

FLOWER CABINET

Approximate size (in.): 32 x 44 x 16
Materials: white oak, red oak, walnut, mahogany

P.O. Box 803
Fort Bragg, CA 95437
(707) 961-1707

DESIGN CHARGES:	inquire
DEPOSIT:	30%–50% with balance paid out per agreement
LEAD TIME:	inquire
LOCAL DELIVERY:	inquire
LONG DISTANCE:	best available shipper, plus crating charge

Jeff Lind, Fine Woodworking

"While I admire Shaker, Arts and Crafts, Federal, Queen Anne, and some contemporary styles, I'm not wedded to any particular one. My own style is a synthesis of all I admire."

JEFF LIND recognizes that custom furniture making is about much more than the tangible expression of the craftsman's aesthetic judgement. It is also about satisfying a client's needs. In this connection, Lind encourages a sharing of drawings, photos, and descriptions with each client in order to achieve an end result that is pleasing to both himself and the client.

For 27 years, Lind has worked alone, taking each piece of furniture that passes through his doors from conception to completion by himself. He prefers working with solid wood, particularly figured cherry, maple, walnut, oak, and mahogany. He assembles his furniture using traditional tools and joinery.

His work has appeared in a number of juried shows in Maine and neighboring states.

DINING CHAIR WITH UPHOLSTERED SEAT
Approximate size (in.): 34 x 18 x 20
Materials: cherry, curly maple, upholstery

SOFA CABINET
Approximate size (in.): 27 x 84 x 18
Materials: cherry, bird's-eye maple, walnut

COFFEE TABLE
Approximate size (in.): 18 x 36 x 18
Materials: cherry, curly maple

SOFA TABLE
Approximate size (in.): 30 x 72 x 18
Materials: cherry, curly maple

505 Emery's Bridge Rd.
S. Berwick, ME 03908
(207) 384-2621
jeff@jefflind.com
www.jefflind.com

DESIGN CHARGES:	inquire
DEPOSIT:	50% with balance due on completion
LEAD TIME:	1–6 months
LOCAL DELIVERY:	inquire
LONG DISTANCE:	blanket-wrap shipper, plus crating charge

Jesse Woodworks

"Somewhere, 300 years from now, someone will turn over one of our pieces, see our signatures, and marvel at the wood and the craftsmanship."

MICHAEL AND REBECCA JESSE are building for the future. They believe their designs and construction techniques produce furniture that will endure both structurally and aesthetically for many generations.

Working with native woods and using a combination of traditional and contemporary joinery techniques, the Jesses create furniture that has strong period roots but also expresses a contemporary sensibility. when creating their original work they call upon experience working in Queen Anne, Federal, Art Deco, Biedermeier, Shaker, and Craftsman styles.

Their work is exhibited throughout the Northwest, as well as in galleries in other parts of the nation. In addition, their furniture has appeared in many regional and national publications.

BLANKET CHESTS
Approximate size (in.): 18 x 18 x 42 (each)
Materials: maple, walnut, red oak, various
    species in marquetry (sculptural marquetry
    by Tom Allen)

BEDROOM SET
Approximate sizes (in.): king-size bed,
    26 x 24 x 20 (each nightstand),
    58 x 60 x 21 (chest)
Materials: red oak, wenge, various
    species in marquetry (sculptural
    marquetry by Tom Allen)

ART-STORAGE CABINET

Approximate size (in.): 50 x 42 x 28
Materials: rosewood, ebony, mother-of-pearl, brass

Michael and Rebecca Jesse
P. O. Box 15075
Salem, OR 97309
(503) 370-9183
FAX (503) 370-9183
jesseww@jessewoodworks.com
www.jessewoodworks.com

DESIGN CHARGES:	$200 per piece rolled into purchase price
DEPOSIT:	50% with balance due on completion
LEAD TIME:	5–7 months
LOCAL DELIVERY:	free
LONG DISTANCE:	best available shipper, plus crating charge

J. Miller Handcrafted Furniture

"I work in a wide range of styles, mostly inspired by an aesthetic of elegant simplicity. My own designs have roots in a variety of historic styles and forms, but the interpretations have a contemporary feel."

JEFF MILLER likens a successful piece of furniture to a successful piece of music. "I feel that all the elements that go into a piece of furniture should be in the service of the overall design, much as all the details of a musical performance must serve the piece of music as a whole," he says.

Working with mostly solid woods and using traditional joinery, Miller patiently tunes every element of every piece that passes through his shop. The payoff for this attention to detail has been the acceptance of his work by his clientele, the woodworking press, and the gallery community. Miller has written several woodworking books, including *Beds* (The Taunton Press, 1999), and has appeared in woodworking videos and on television. In addition, his work has been featured in galleries and museums in the Chicago area.

TABLE
Approximate size (in.): 30 x 45 x 24
Materials: bird's-eye maple, maple,
   purpleheart

CONSOLE TABLE
Approximate size (in.): 32 x 62 x 15
Materials: cherry, black resin

ROCKING CHAIR
Approximate size (in.): 41 x 25 x 41
Material: maple

CHAIR
Approximate size (in.): 44 x 20 x 20 (each)
Materials: cherry (or walnut), black resin

TABLE
Approximate size (in.):
18 x 18 x 18
Material: mahogany

Jeff Miller
1774 W. Lunt Ave.
Chicago, IL 60626
(773) 761-3311
FAX (773) 761-7546
jeff@furnituremaking.com
www.furnituremaking.com

DESIGN CHARGES:	none
DEPOSIT:	50% with balance due on completion
LEAD TIME:	4–7 months
LOCAL DELIVERY:	usually $75–$100
LONG DISTANCE:	blanket-wrap carrier or crated and sent common carrier

JoAnn Schuch Woodworking

"I design original pieces for each situation. Whether it is one special furnishing or several coordinated pieces, I work closely with the client or the interior designer."

JoAnn Schuch stole her way into the woodworking field. After graduating from Pitzer College with a B.A. in art and completing some graduate work in bronze figurative sculpture, Schuch visited a show of Arts and Crafts-style furniture. While there, she covertly took the measurements of a Morris chair and proceeded to build a copy using only a hammer, a chisel, and a dovetail saw.

Today she practices her woodworking out in the open, running a shop with two employees where she creates furniture she describes as "a conscious meditation on beauty." She works primarily with solid wood using traditional joinery, although she does use veneers and plywood if a piece calls for it. Her work has appeared on the pages of *Woodwork* magazine and *Woodshop News,* as well as in the book *Going Professional: A Woodworker's Guide* by Jim Tolpin (Linden Publishing).

"RUNNING DOG" AUDIO CABINET
Approximate size (in.): 40 x 28 x 22
Materials: maple, walnut

GREENE AND GREENE DINING-ROOM TABLE
Approximate size (in.): 30 x 40 x 78
Materials: cherry, ebony

TANSU DRESSER
Approximate size (in.): 60 x 54 x 23
Material: walnut

MORRIS RECLINER
Approximate size (in.): 44 x 28 x 34
Material: cherry

1111 Hoffman Rd.
McKinleyville, CA 95519
(707) 839-0147
FAX (707) 839-0147
jschuch@reninet.com
www.woodguild.com/schuch

DESIGN CHARGES:	$50 per hour rolled into purchase price if total design time is less than two hours
DEPOSIT:	50% with balance due on completion for orders less than $3,000; 33% at signing, 33% at start of construction, and balance due on completion for orders more than $3,000
LEAD TIME:	3–6 months
LOCAL DELIVERY:	free
LONG DISTANCE:	16% of purchase price

John A. Kapel Design

"Chairs are in essence useful, freestanding sculptures."

JOHN KAPEL'S approach to woodworking is based upon the notion of doing the most with the least. As he practices it, the process of design is more about subtraction than addition. He winnows out superfluous elements, a distillation that leaves behind only what is structurally and visually essential.

Unlike many designers/craftsmen, Kapel doesn't have a catalog of pieces from which his clients may choose. Each piece that leaves his shop is one of a kind, custom designed to suit a particular client's needs and tastes.

Trained as an industrial designer at the Cranbrook Academy in Michigan, Kapel also studied metal design at the University of Copenhagen before teaching himself woodworking. Much of the creative output of his 45-year career has been in the form of prototype furniture, which was then manufactured by companies in the United States and Japan.

His work has appeared in museums and exhibitions throughout the country, as well as in Paris.

DINING CHAIR
Approximate size (in.): 34 x 22 x 21
Material: cherry

STOOL
Approximate size (in.): 16 x 24 x 18
Material: cherry

DESK CHAIR
Approximate size (in.): 36 x 21 x 20
Material: walnut

DINING CHAIR
Approximate size (in.): 34 x 22 x 21
Material: walnut, leather, cane

80 Skywood Way
Woodside, CA 94062
(650) 851-0888
FAX (650) 851-8060
www.johnkapel.com

DESIGN CHARGES:	$150 per hour rolled into purchase price
DEPOSIT:	none
LEAD TIME:	inquire
LOCAL DELIVERY:	free
LONG DISTANCE:	best available shipper, no crating charge

John Houck/Studio Furniture

"I think people's lives are enhanced by living in beautiful surroundings, and furniture is as important as painting or sculpture in achieving that enhancement."

JOHN HOUCK does no reproduction work, nor does he do any production-run work. Each piece produced in his shop is an original, built one at a time, destined either for gallery display or to meet a client's particular needs.

Houck believes that art has the capacity to enrich people's lives, and his definition of art is broad enough to include the functional arts, such as furniture. In fact, he sees furniture as a more "responsible medium" than painting or sculpture because furniture must meet rigorous standards of functionality and durability, as well as be beautiful.

Houck prefers working in solid wood of domestic origins, although he has occasionally succumbed to the temptation to use tropical imports. Many of the wood species he uses require no finish, but when a finish is required, he uses shellac or a water-based finish.

He has shown his work in a number of exhibitions, ranging from his home base in Los Angeles to Boston.

SHOE CABINET
Approximate size (in.): 54 x 32 x 19
Materials: basswood, cocobolo, ebony, silk

LAMP
Approximate size (in.): 8 x 6 x 14
Materials: purpleheart, maple, glass

TABLE

Approximate size (in.): 30 x 48 x 94
Material: pine

CHEST OF DRAWERS

Approximate size (in.): 70 x 26 x 22
Material: maple

3654 Grand View Blvd.
Los Angeles, CA 90066
(310) 397-7993
FAX (310) 397-0274
famous8a@aol.com

DESIGN CHARGES:	none
DEPOSIT:	33% with balance due on completion
LEAD TIME:	1½–2 months
LOCAL DELIVERY:	free, unless truck hire is required
LONG DISTANCE:	UPS or air freight, plus crating charge

J. P. Callahan, Ltd. LLC

"Our aim is to build pieces of extraordinary beauty and charm, whatever the style."

ALTHOUGH HIS PRODUCT LINE is expanding, J. P. Callahan's business is built on a single, sturdy foundation: the reproduction of 18th-century scallop-shell, barrel-back corner cupboards. While some might find such specialization confining, Callahan has created a wide variety of choices within this tightly defined realm, offering his buyers a number of styles, woods, and finishes. He is now adding millwork to his repertoire as well as some free-standing casepieces that are not in the corner-cupboard genre.

Callahan's shop methods emphasize handwork: All dovetails are cut by hand, all shells are carved by hand, and many surfaces are created using hand-planes. In addition, the finish on all stained work is hand-padded shellac. This labor-intensive approach ensures not only the historical accuracy of the finished work but also imparts a texture that machine processes can't approximate.

TIGER MAPLE CORNER CUPBOARD
Approximate size (in.): 85 x 42 x 31
Materials: tiger maple, pine

COUNTRY FRENCH CORNER CUPBOARD
Approximate size (in.): 85 x 54 x 38
Materials: poplar, pine

PAINTED CORNER CUPBOARD

Approximate size (in.): 85 x 42 x 30
Material: pine

PALLADIAN CORNER CUPBOARD

Approximate size (in.): 91 x 42 x 31
Materials: tiger maple, pine

John Callahan
56 Bridlewood Rd.
South Windsor, CT 06074
(800) 582-1788
(860) 644-5879
jcall77176@aol.com

DESIGN CHARGES:	$25 per hour rolled into purchase price
DEPOSIT:	$500, with 50% of balance paid at the halfway point and the remainder paid on completion
LEAD TIME:	3–6 months
LOCAL DELIVERY:	free
LONG DISTANCE:	best available shipper, plus crating charge

Kent James Odell Furniture

"Thousands of decisions are required in the making of a single piece of furniture... success lies in making these decisions artfully."

KENT JAMES ODELL takes an eclectic approach to woodworking. Stylistically, his taste runs from Ruhlman to Wright, from Queen Anne to Greene and Greene. This openness to diversity also asserts itself in his shop practices. He assembles much of his furniture using traditional joinery, but he's not opposed to using such 20th-century technology as the vacuum press.

Odell began his study of woodworking as a cabinetmaking apprentice to Juan Pomes in New York City. From Pomes, Odell learned that a good cabinetmaker never knows it all, a philosophy that has left Odell open to the prospect of learning not only from historical masters but also from other modern designers who bring their ideas to him to build.

In 1983 Odell went out on his own, then two years later he decided to concentrate on private commissions for fine furniture.

CABINET
Approximate size (in.): 33 x 20 x 14
Material: bubinga

SIDEBOARD
Approximate size (in.): 38 x 69 x 23
Materials: sycamore, birch, Corian, silk

COCKTAIL TABLE
Approximate size (in.): 19 x 22
Materials: maple, Corian

CHAIR
Approximate size (in.): 35 x 22 x 20
Materials: bubinga, leather

3001 Bayshore Rd. #10
Benicia, CA 94510
(707) 747-1337
kjodell@pacbell.net
www.odellfurniture.com

DESIGN CHARGES:	inquire
DEPOSIT:	50% with balance due on completion
LEAD TIME:	2–3 months
LOCAL DELIVERY:	usually free
LONG DISTANCE:	freight company, plus crating charge

Kevin Kopil Furniture Design

"I have found my customers are drawn to the elegant simplicity of my work. They realize they have purchased an heirloom that will last generations."

KEVIN KOPIL'S first line of original furniture was rooted in the Shaker aesthetic, although he added delicate curves and tapers to give the pieces more warmth and spirit. His second line, which he called the Floating World, was inspired by the work of Frank Lloyd Wright. Here, too, Kopil couldn't resist tinkering with the original designs, adding ebony slats, spindles, and dovetails, as well as "floating" tops. These elements—some of which can be seen in the furniture shown at right—give a Japanese flavor to Kopil's work.

Kopil uses domestic hardwoods, favoring cherry, figured maple, and walnut. He assembles his work with a wide range of joinery, including mortise and tenon, splines, and dowels.

Kopil began working with wood at age 10 and honed his talents by working in apprenticeship programs with master craftsmen. He has exhibited in many juried shows on the East Coast. His work has also appeared in several national woodworking magazines.

TABLE
Approximate size (in.): 30 x 46 x 96
Materials: cherry, walnut, wenge

BED
Approximate size (in.): 52 x 80 x 76
Materials: cherry, walnut

SIDEBOARD
Approximate size (in.): 36 x 23 x 72
Materials: cherry, walnut, wenge

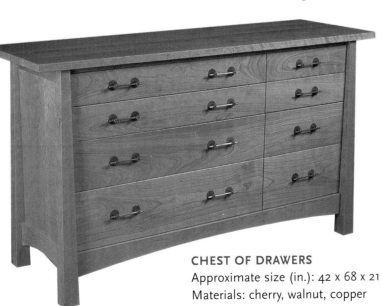

CHEST OF DRAWERS
Approximate size (in.): 42 x 68 x 21
Materials: cherry, walnut, copper

P. O. Box 411, Rte. 2
Jonesville, VT 05466
(802) 434-4400
FAX (802) 434-5639
kkopil@together.net
www.kevinkopil.com

DESIGN CHARGES: $100
DEPOSIT: 50% with balance due
                  on completion
LEAD TIME: 2–3 months
LOCAL DELIVERY: free
LONG DISTANCE: blanket-wrap shipper

The Kingswood Shop

"I draw constant inspiration from contemporary and historical precedents in the arenas of furniture and architectural design."

MOST INDEPENDENT FURNITURE MAKERS handpick the material they use in their work, but not all go as deeply into that process as Peter Naramore. In addition to choosing his material, he also dries it and in some cases participates in the logging of the timber from which that material will be cut.

Working primarily in koa, a species found only in Hawaii, Naramore builds in a broad range of styles. Thirty years as a designer/craftsman have given him the confidence to move in and out of many stylistic traditions.

He has exhibited in galleries on Maui and Oahu. His work has also appeared on the pages of the last four volumes of the *Design Book* series published by The Taunton Press.

DETAIL

DESK
Approximate size (in.): 30 x 66 x 33
Materials: koa, siricote

LADIES' WRITING DESK
Approximate size (in.):
30 x 42 x 28
Materials: curly koa,
lacewood, ebony

DETAIL

ENTRY TABLE
Approximate size (in.): 29 x 52 x 15
Material: curly koa

Peter Naramore
R. R. #2, Box 214
Kula, HI 96790
(808) 878-3626
FAX (808) 878-3626
trigger@maui.net

DESIGN CHARGES:	$200–$400 per piece, not rolled into purchase price
DEPOSIT:	50% with balance due on completion
LEAD TIME:	6–12 months
LOCAL DELIVERY:	free on island of Maui
LONG DISTANCE:	best available shipper, plus crating charge

Kinloch Woodworking

"We can do anything. We have the wood inventory and skills to back up that claim. From Newport desks to orchid inlays for a Hinckley sailboat, when customers want the best, they visit us."

D. DOUGLAS MOOBERRY speaks with unabashed enthusiasm about the quality of the work that leaves his shop. He offers clients ". . . amazing wood, great craftsmanship. . . with skills and wood inventory to blow away any style." He attributes his ability to attract and retain top-quality cabinetmakers to outstanding working conditions and benefits.

After receiving a business degree from Gettysburg College, Mooberry apprenticed under a woodworker before opening his own shop. Since that time, he and the cabinetmakers in his employ have continued their education by taking courses from, among others, Sam Maloof and the staff at the Winterthur Museum in Delaware.

The work of his shop has been the subject of dozens of articles in newspapers, books, and magazines, including *Fine Woodworking, Home Furniture, Colonial Homes Magazine,* and *Art Matters.*

NEWPORT SECRETARY DESK
Approximate size (in.): 104 x 42 x 22
Material: quilted mahogany

CHIPPENDALE CABINETS
Approximate size (in.): 108 x 41 x 20 (each)
Material: mahogany

CORNER CABINET
Approximate size (in.): 88 x 34 x 20
Materials: curly cherry, tiger maple

PIECRUST TEA TABLE
Approximate size (in.): 28 x 36
Material: mahogany

D. Douglas Mooberry
P. O. Box 461
Unionville, PA 19375
(610) 347-2070
FAX (610) 347-0353
kinloch@kennett.net
www.kinlochwoodworking.com

DESIGN CHARGES:	$75 per hour rolled into purchase price
DEPOSIT:	50% with balance due on completion
LEAD TIME:	6 months
LOCAL DELIVERY:	free
LONG DISTANCE:	inquire

Don Kondra

"I like to think of myself more as a craftsman than as an artist. I don't wax philosophical about my work: I just do it."

ALTHOUGH HE OCCASIONALLY builds furniture on speculation, Don Kondra prefers collaborating with a client on the design of a piece intended to suit that client's needs. In particular, he enjoys the craftsman/client relationship that develops during this process—a relationship Kondra believes inspires him to invest himself most fully in the creative process.

Kondra, a self-taught woodworker, builds contemporary furniture using traditional methods, working with both solid wood and veneers. Although he uses the best available materials and techniques and although he insists on maintaining the highest standards of quality, Kondra sees himself as more of a craftsman than as an artist.

Kondra is a two-time winner of Saskatchewan's most prestigious craft award, and in 1998 *Western Living* magazine named him one of the top 50 designers in Western Canada. His work has also appeared in many other Canadian and American publications.

BLANKET CHEST
Approximate size (in.): 27 x 40 x 17
Materials: walnut, walnut burl, Baltic birch

SIDEBOARD

Approximate size (in.):
32 x 52 x 20
Materials: various
rosewoods, birch

DETAIL

STEREO CABINET

Approximate size (in.): 28 x 50 x 20
Material: cherry

R. R. #2, Site 1, Box 73
Saskatoon, Saskatchewan,
Canada S7K 3J5
(306) 382-7385
donkondra@sk.sympatico.ca
www3.sk.sympatico.ca/donkon/

DESIGN CHARGES:	$30 per hour rolled into purchase price
DEPOSIT:	50% with balance due on completion
LEAD TIME:	4–12 months
LOCAL DELIVERY:	free
LONG DISTANCE:	UPS or ground transport, plus crating charge

Kurt Gutbier Woodworking

"My goal is to build reproduction furniture that has the construction, material, style, and finish found on pieces built a century or more ago."

ALTHOUGH KURT GUTBIER specializes in exact reproductions of period originals, he also enjoys working with clients to create completely new, one-of-a-kind pieces to suit their particular needs. His only requirement is that those one-of-a-kind pieces remain true to the historical traditions within which he works.

In Gutbier's shop, the drive for historical accuracy goes beyond the use of measured drawings of specific originals. He insists on employing traditional joinery, such as mortise and tenon and hand-cut dovetails, as well as using traditional handplaned surface preparations. In addition, Gutbier employs finishing techniques that mimic the appearance of worn (even abused) surfaces.

His work has appeared in the Weston Craft Show in Weston, Vermont, as well as on the pages of the *Dorset County Journal* and *Manchester Journal*.

LINEN PRESS
Approximate size (in.): 84 x 42 x 26
Material: cherry

HANGING CORNER CUPBOARD
Approximate size (in.): 32 x 15 x 12
Material: poplar

DETAIL

TRESTLE-BASE,
GATE-LEG COFFEE TABLE
Approximate size (in.): 18 x 32 x 42
Materials: pine, maple

R. R. #1, Box 1816
Pawlet, VT 05761
(802) 325-6252
kurtanddenise@aol.com

DESIGN CHARGES:	none
DEPOSIT:	30% with balance due on completion
LEAD TIME:	2–3 months
LOCAL DELIVERY:	free within 50 miles
LONG DISTANCE:	best available shipper, plus crating charge

Kurt Piper Woodworking

"I feel that custom furniture has a unique potential to have an impact on the quality and enjoyment of life for a broader range of individuals than was true in the recent past."

KURT PIPER begins with a design that is both "cohesive and sensible," then he executes that design with the finest available materials. Sometimes those materials are as familiar as cherry and maple. Other times, however, Piper introduces materials not typically associated with furniture: steel, petrified wood, and kangaroo hide.

Piper began his training at a summer program in artisanship at Boston University in 1978 before apprenticing with Timothy Philbrick (see p. 232). Although he describes his formal education as limited, he has built a substantial woodworking library, and he continually strives to improve himself as a furniture maker through self-directed education.

His work has been accepted into juried shows and featured in several national and regional publications. In addition, he received the Travel Stipend Award conferred by the Philadelphia Furnishings Show, which permitted him to study Art Nouveau and Art Deco furniture in France.

KORRI'S MUSIC STAND
Approximate size (in.): 30 x 19 x 11
Materials: cherry, curly maple

ADJUSTABLE MUSIC STAND
Approximate size (in.): 52–57 x 15 x 12
Materials: cherry, curly maple, ebony

ARCHITECT'S STOOL
Approximate size (in.): 29 x 19 x 11
Materials: cherry, maple, ebony

SPIDER TABLE
Approximate size (in.): 20 x 28
Materials: maple, slate, kangaroo hide

34 Front St.
P. O. Box 51502
Indian Orchard, MA 01151
(413) 543-8779
FAX (413) 543-5783
piperwoodworking@juno.com

DESIGN CHARGES:	$75 per hour rolled into purchase price
DEPOSIT:	33%–50% with balance due on completion
LEAD TIME:	6–9 months
LOCAL DELIVERY:	inquire
LONG DISTANCE:	best available shipper, plus crating charge

Lawrence J. Perna, Antiques

"My focus on Federal period furniture has become my occupation."

LARRY PERNA began his career the same way as the 18th- and 19th-century designers/craftsmen who serve as his inspiration: as an apprentice in a cabinet shop, receiving hands-on training from experienced craftsmen. This early instruction, followed by 22 years of experience as a furniture maker, has equipped Perna with an intimate knowledge of furniture design and construction.

Perna specializes in high-style period furniture, in particular Federal furniture of the Hepplewhite period. Perna's work therefore often employs the characteristic features of Hepplewhite work: mahogany, inlays, hand-cut joinery, and a hand-rubbed finish. He believes that the furniture of this period has a "timelessness of design that fits into today's lifestyle as if it were new."

His work has been featured in *Design Times* magazine.

HEPPLEWHITE-STYLE PEMBROKE TABLE
Approximate size (in.): 30 x 20 x 28
Materials: mahogany, maple, poplar

CHINESE-STYLE COCKTAIL TABLE
Approximate size (in.): 18 x 30 x 42
Material: mahogany

FEDERAL-STYLE FLIP-TOP CARD TABLE
Approximate size (in.): 30 x 36 x 18 (plus leaf)
Materials: mahogany, satinwood

243 South St.
Medfield, MA 02052
(508) 359-5347

DESIGN CHARGES:	inquire
DEPOSIT:	50% with balance due on completion
LEAD TIME:	6–12 months
LOCAL DELIVERY:	inquire
LONG DISTANCE:	best available shipper, plus crating charge

LeFort Fine Furniture

"Our customers are generally knowledgeable about the best period furniture and rely on us to pass on the rich legacy of past furniture makers."

THE PURCHASE of a Cape Cod house built in 1720 whetted David LeFort's appetite for period furniture. That led him to begin purchasing—and later selling—period originals. He then took the next logical step: building his own period furniture, focusing on historical accuracy, fine materials, and traditional joinery. After showing some of his earliest work at the Fogg Art Museum at Harvard University, he made the transition to full-time furniture construction.

LeFort believes that the "bench cabinetmaker" system he uses ensures the most successful furniture construction in a shop like his in which much of the furniture is built by employees. This system requires a single cabinetmaker to follow a project from beginning to end, assuming full responsibility for the ultimate quality of that piece.

And his system works. LeFort's furniture has been the subject of articles in *Early American Life*, *Traditional Home Decorator Showcase*, and *South Shore Magazine*. In addition, his work has been shown in many locations in the eastern United States.

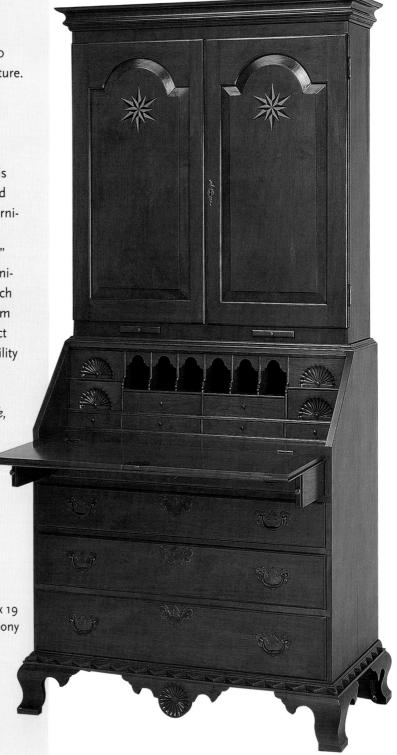

DUNLAP SECRETARY WITH INLAID COMPASS STARS
Approximate size (in.): 79 x 36 x 19
Materials: cherry, satinwood, ebony

NEWPORT CARD TABLE
Approximate size (in.): 30 x 36 x 36
Material: mahogany

OXBOW FOUR-DRAWER CHEST
Approximate size (in.): 32 x 38 x 20
Material: curly birch

THREE-SHELL, SLANT-FRONT DESK
Approximate size (in.): 42 x 42 x 23
Material: mahogany

David LeFort
293 Winter St.
Hanover, MA 02339
(781) 826-9033
(781) 826-9094
lefort@tiac.net
www.lefortfurnituremakers.com

DESIGN CHARGES:	inquire
DEPOSIT:	50% with balance due on completion
LEAD TIME:	2–9 months
LOCAL DELIVERY:	inquire
LONG DISTANCE:	blanket-wrap shipper

Lutkus III Design

"Inspired by the Arts and Crafts and Art Deco movements and the lessons of their founders, I work to continue the evolution of America's most notable era of design."

CHARLES LUTKUS has staked his claim on a category of furniture that is often overlooked by professional woodworkers: lighting. Although he does build other kinds of pieces—tables, desks, and shelves, for example—his focus is on woodwork that illuminates. In fact, lighting is often a key element in the design of his desks.

Working alone, Lutkus builds his Arts and Crafts- and Art Deco-inspired designs from cherry using biscuit and dowel joinery. He prefers working with cherry because its fine grain permits the execution of detailed accents. He then gives the completed pieces a satin urethane finish.

Lutkus's work has appeared in broadcast and newspaper coverage in the Dallas area and has been selected for presentation at an industry trade show in Las Vegas.

FOREST PARK TORCHÈRE
Approximate size (in.): 71 x 18 x 18
Materials: cherry, glass

ITASCA TABLE TORCHÈRE
Approximate size (in.): 25 x 13 x 13
Materials: cherry, glass

FOREST PARK
FLOOR LAMP
Approximate size (in.):
61 x 18 x 18
Materials: cherry, glass

MULLINS DESK
Approximate size (in.): 55 x 36 x 24
Materials: cherry, glass

Charles Lutkus
6 Forest Park Dr.
Richardson, TX 75080
(972) 231-9865
FAX (972) 479-9483
lutkus3@aol.com

DESIGN CHARGES:	inquire
DEPOSIT:	25%–50% with balance due on completion
LEAD TIME:	1–3 months
LOCAL DELIVERY:	inquire
LONG DISTANCE:	best available shipper

Mack and Rodel Studio

"By allowing the clients to become involved in the process, I can function as their hands and thereby further add to their appreciation of the final product."

IN 1990 KEVIN P. RODEL decided to build only Arts and Crafts-style furniture. But instead of feeling confined by this choice, he has found the style to be so broad and diverse that "new concepts and nuances are constantly being uncovered." Some of Rodel's work consists of reproductions of specific Arts and Crafts originals, but more often his furniture is a contemporary reinterpretation of Arts and Crafts forms and motifs created in collaboration with his clients.

Rodel's work has appeared on the pages of *Home Furniture* and *Fine Woodworking* magazines. He is currently at work on a book for The Taunton Press tentatively entitled *The Craftsman Legacy*, which explores Arts and Crafts-style furniture.

DETAIL

DESK
Approximate size (in.): 30 x 72 x 33
Materials: white oak, ebony, leather

DETAIL

BOOKCASE
Approximate size (in.): 38 x 54 x 18
Materials: cherry, maple, oak, pewter, glass, copper

SIDEBOARD
Approximate size (in.): 40 x 70 x 22
Materials: cherry, maple, copper

Kevin P. Rodel
44 Leighton Rd.
Pownal, ME 04069
(207) 688-4483
macrodel@aol.com
www.neaguild.com/macrodel

DESIGN CHARGES:	$100–$300 rolled into purchase price
DEPOSIT:	25% with balance due on completion
LEAD TIME:	8–12 months
LOCAL DELIVERY:	free within 30 miles
LONG DISTANCE:	inquire

Mack S. Headley and Sons

"Since the early 1920s, we have been in the business of studying, restoring, reproducing, and selling period pieces of American furniture."

IN A TIME when most American furniture makers enter the field after first sampling other careers, Mack S. Headley and Sons is an anomaly: It is a family business with a continuous pedigree that extends 80 years into the past. Jeff L. Headley, who with the help of his partner, Steve Hamilton, now runs the company, is training the fifth-generation Headley to work in this furniture-making business.

The Headleys have enjoyed hands-on access to the original pieces they reproduce, which gives them "a better feel for the lines, construction, and proportions, which translates into a better piece of furniture."

Mack S. Headley and Sons has a distinguished client list that includes many heads of state, West Point, and many museums. The firm's work has appeared in *Southern Accents*, *Architectural Digest*, and *Colonial Homes* magazine, among others.

SHERATON WRITING DESK
Approximate size (in.): 30 x 40 x 21
Materials: mahogany, curly maple, boxwood, ebony, yellow pine

CHEST-ON-CHEST
Approximate size (in.): 85 x 42 x 22
Materials: cherry, poplar

HIGH CHEST OF DRAWERS
Approximate size (in.): 66 x 44 x 23
Materials: cherry, poplar

SIDEBOARD
Approximate size (in.): 40 x 66 x 23
Materials: mahogany, poplar

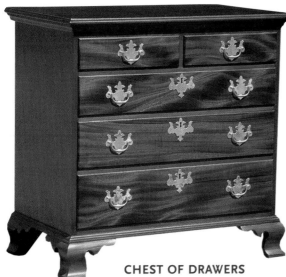

CHEST OF DRAWERS
Approximate size (in.): 34 x 35 x 21

Jeff L. Headley/Steve Hamilton
217 Helmley Ln.
Berryville, VA 22611
(540) 955-2022
jheadley@shentel.net

DESIGN CHARGES:	$40 per hour usually rolled into purchase price
DEPOSIT:	25% with balance due on completion
LEAD TIME:	12–18 months
LOCAL DELIVERY:	free
LONG DISTANCE:	small pieces shipped Fed Ex or UPS; inquire about large pieces

Mark Levin Studio

"Some designs take years to define themselves while others come through within the first rendition."

MARK LEVIN'S approach to the design process is different from that of most furniture makers. He begins by visualizing not a construction in wood but a construction in an imaginary matte black, monolithic material. If the form works in that material, Levin believes it will be even more powerful when wrought in wood.

He prefers solid wood to veneers because "the material in its solid form has more sexiness, intrinsic value...." He assembles his work using traditional joinery, then finishes with either oil or polyurethane, depending on the function of the piece.

Levin has exhibited throughout the Midwest. He has also earned a large number of corporate and ecclesiastical commissions.

LEAF TABLE #20
Approximate size (in.):
28 x 52 x 24
Material: red alder

NYMPH BENCH
Approximate size (in.):
17 x 54 x 12
Materials: red oak, walnut

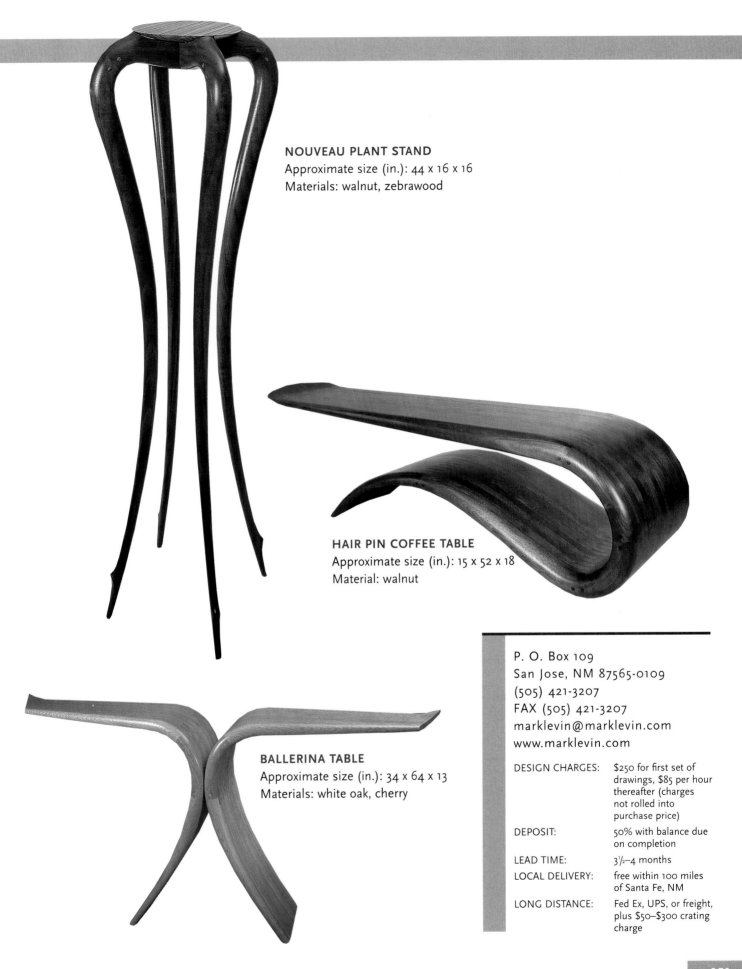

NOUVEAU PLANT STAND
Approximate size (in.): 44 x 16 x 16
Materials: walnut, zebrawood

HAIR PIN COFFEE TABLE
Approximate size (in.): 15 x 52 x 18
Material: walnut

BALLERINA TABLE
Approximate size (in.): 34 x 64 x 13
Materials: white oak, cherry

P. O. Box 109
San Jose, NM 87565-0109
(505) 421-3207
FAX (505) 421-3207
marklevin@marklevin.com
www.marklevin.com

DESIGN CHARGES:	$250 for first set of drawings, $85 per hour thereafter (charges not rolled into purchase price)
DEPOSIT:	50% with balance due on completion
LEAD TIME:	3½–4 months
LOCAL DELIVERY:	free within 100 miles of Santa Fe, NM
LONG DISTANCE:	Fed Ex, UPS, or freight, plus $50–$300 crating charge

The Master's Touch

"I have great respect for the genius of 18th-century cabinetmakers because their construction methods have endured for more than 200 years."

THIRTY YEARS AGO, Ralph Jensen began his training in the shop of Otto Zenke of Greensboro, North Carolina, studying the design and execution of new custom work as well as the restoration of period originals. Since then, his woodworking education has continued through self-directed study and participation in many woodworking seminars.

Jensen believes that the study of period originals enables him to think like the craftsmen who created those originals. He then applies this thought process to the creation of new work, which he is convinced will become the antique treasures of the future.

His work has been featured in many local periodicals and several national magazines as well as on regional television.

ELIPHALET CHAPIN CONNECTICUT HIGHBOY
Approximate size (in.): 96 x 42 x 22
Material: mahogany

17TH-CENTURY-STYLE PANEL-BOTTOM CHAIRS
Approximate size (in.): 40 x 24 x 18 (each)
Material: white oak

18TH-CENTURY-STYLE SCROLL-TOP EAGLE HIGHBOY
Approximate size (in.): 113 x 42 x 22
Material: mahogany

DETAIL

Ralph Jensen
300 Old Dairy Rd.
Wilmington, NC 28405
(910) 799-4545
FAX (910) 799-8443
masters@issac.net
www.mastershoppe.com

DESIGN CHARGES:	none
DEPOSIT:	inquire
LEAD TIME:	1½–3 months
LOCAL DELIVERY:	free
LONG DISTANCE:	best available shipper, plus crating charge

Harv Mastalir

"For me, woodworking is a continuous exploration of material, form, and function. My work reflects this personal inquiry into wood, technique, and design."

A SELF-TAUGHT designer/craftsman, Harv Mastalir describes his designs as modest. "I strive for clean, elegant lines and simplicity, incorporating quiet details and accents to enhance visual vitality."

Mastalir works with both solid wood and veneers. His construction techniques are traditional, relying on mortise-and-tenon joints and hand-cut dovetails.

In the 15 years since he set out as a full-time furniture maker, his work has been named the Best of Show three times at the Woodworking Exhibition sponsored by the Woodworker's Guild of Colorado Springs. In addition, Mastalir has served on the faculty at the Center for Furniture Craftsmanship at Rockport, Maine; the Anderson Ranch Arts Center in Snowmass, Colorado; and Red Rocks Community College of Lakewood, Colorado.

DINING TABLE WITH LEAVES
Approximate size (in.): 30 x 87
Materials: walnut, maple

DETAIL

DETAIL

SIDEBOARD AND LIQUOR CABINET
Approximate sizes (in.): 36 x 48 x 21 (sideboard),
36 x 30 x 15 (liquor cabinet)
Materials: cherry, bird's-eye maple

WOVEN-TOP HALL TABLE
Approximate size (in.): 34 x 54 x 14
Materials: cherry, ash, ebony

3024 Valmont
Boulder, CO 80301
(303) 449-2552
FAX (720) 304-7389
Harvmastalir@hotmail.com

DESIGN CHARGES:	$300–$500 rolled into purchase price
DEPOSIT:	50% with balance due on completion
LEAD TIME:	6–9 months
LOCAL DELIVERY:	free
LONG DISTANCE:	blanket-wrap shipper, plus crating charge

Maynard and Maynard Furnituremakers

"The bottom line with our company is that we work hard to maintain quality while keeping the furniture accessible to the broad public."

PETER MAYNARD'S 25 years as a designer/craftsman have equipped him with a broad knowledge of furniture styles and technical skills. He feels comfortable taking a commission that reflects almost any stylistic category. He feels similarly confident about his skills, which include traditional joinery techniques as well as methods appropriate for contemporary materials such as advanced lamination technology. In addition, Maynard often integrates nonwood materials into his work, favoring brass, stone, and glass.

Maynard's furniture has been featured in many national magazines, such as *Architectural Digest, Interior Design Magazine,* and *Woodwork.* Also, *Traditional Home* magazine presented Maynard's work in an article entitled "20th-Century Masters: Five of the Country's Best Furniture Makers."

SIDEBOARD
Approximate size (in.): 32 x 48 x 20
Materials: walnut, various other woods

DETAIL

HAND-CARVED CHINESE TABLE
Approximate size (in.): 30 x 40 x 20
Material: rosewood

CARD TABLE
Approximate size (in.): 30 x 36 x 18
  (36 when opened)
Materials: curly maple, ebony,
  rosewood

Peter and Marcie Maynard
H C 63, Box 141 Beryl Mtn. Rd.
South Acworth, NH 03607
(603) 835-2969
FAX (603) 835-2969
www.classicfinefurniture.com

DESIGN CHARGES:	10% of estimated cost, rolled into purchase price if preceded by a 50% deposit on the entire cost
DEPOSIT:	50% with balance due on completion prior to delivery
LEAD TIME:	3–9 months
LOCAL DELIVERY:	inquire
LONG DISTANCE:	$300–$600

M. C. Seward, Custom Furniture Maker

"My work is characterized by clean lines inspired by Shaker furniture, as well as by the use of hand-selected highly figured wood, carefully arranged to balance and match the wood grain."

MICHAEL SEWARD is a traditionalist, assembling his furniture in much the same way as his 18th- and 19th-century predecessors. He uses mortise-and-tenon joinery and hand-cut dovetails and builds up his finishes with many coats of hand-rubbed oil.

Seward works primarily in native woods traditionally favored by American cabinetmakers: cherry, walnut, and maple. And to give his work a strong sense of visual unity, he sees to it that every bit of wood in a piece of furniture is taken from material harvested from the same log.

He exhibits in galleries throughout Maryland. His work has also been featured in many regional publications, in *This Old House* magazine, as well as in the book *Chest of Drawers* by Bill Hylton (upcoming from The Taunton Press).

FIGURED-WALNUT CHEST ON LEGS
Approximate size (in.): 50 x 28 x 17
Materials: figured walnut, maple

CHEST OF DRAWERS ON LEGS
Approximate size (in.): 38 x 36 x 16
Material: figured cherry

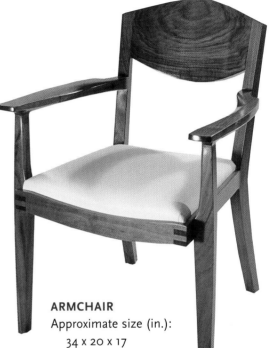

ARMCHAIR
Approximate size (in.):
34 x 20 x 17
Material: black walnut

**SIX-LEG EXTENSION
DINING TABLE**
Approximate size (in.): 30 x 48 x 48
(92 with leaves in place)
Material: walnut

Michael Seward
9706 Manifold Rd.
New Park, PA 17352
(717) 993-9040, (800) 993-9040

DESIGN CHARGES:	$100 rolled into purchase price
DEPOSIT:	$100 design deposit, with balance paid out in thirds as work progresses
LEAD TIME:	6 months
LOCAL DELIVERY:	inquire
LONG DISTANCE:	UPS or common carrier, plus crating charge

Michael Cullen Design

"I enjoy meeting with clients in their homes in order to gain a better understanding of who they are within their own environment."

AFTER 14 YEARS as a professional furniture maker, Michael Cullen has achieved a skill level that permits him to focus more on *what* he will make rather than *how* he will make it. This confidence frees him to focus on the development of his design vocabulary of shapes, textures, and colors—a vocabulary enhanced through his study of nature. He is inspired by the intricate details, the patterns, and the colors that abound in the natural world.

Cullen's work has been exhibited in New York, Chicago, and Miami, as well as in many California venues. It has also appeared in *Home Furniture* magazine and in several of The Taunton Press' *Design Books*.

BLANKET CHEST
Approximate size (in.): 28 x 30 x 16
Materials: painted mahogany, wenge, cedar

CHEST
Approximate size (in.): 12 x 16 x 11
Materials: painted mahogany, redwood lace burl

DISPLAY CASE

Approximate size (in.): 84 x 96 x 20
Materials: maple, pear, glass, painted wood

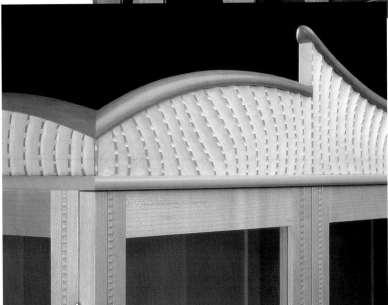

DETAIL

300 North Water St.
Petaluma, CA 94952
(707) 778-6301
FAX (707) 778-6301
michaelcullendesign@msn.com

DESIGN CHARGES:	$300–$500 rolled into purchase price
DEPOSIT:	50% with balance due on completion
LEAD TIME:	2–6 months
LOCAL DELIVERY:	inquire
LONG DISTANCE:	best available shipper

Michael Hoffer Furniture and Design

"I make one-of-a-kind and limited production pieces that reflect my own aesthetic vision. In the case of commission work, I try to meld that vision with the client's needs."

MICHAEL HOFFER identifies several sources of design inspiration for his work, the most important being nature. For example, the shape of a Hoffer table leg might be suggested by an animal tusk or a flower emerging from its sheath. His work also reflects the influences of the early 20th-century's Art Deco and Arts and Crafts movements, as well as oriental design.

Hoffer prepared for a career as a furniture maker by attending the California College of Arts and Crafts and the College of the Redwoods, which equipped him with the requisite knowledge of materials and joinery. In this regard, he is very much a traditionalist, relying on mortise-and-tenon, dovetail, and frame-and-panel construction.

Hoffer's work has appeared in *Design Book Seven* and *Built-In Furniture* (both from The Taunton Press). In addition, his work has been shown in galleries and juried exhibitions throughout the western United States.

DETAIL

JEWELRY CABINET
Approximate size (in.): 54 x 14 x 14
Materials: mahogany, bird's-eye and
quilted maple, ebony, bone

TUSK TABLE #1
Approximate size (in.): 30 x 42 x 14
Materials: sycamore, ash, holly

SCREEN
Approximate size (in.): 68 x 66 x 1
Materials: cherry, bamboo paper

DINING CHAIRS
Approximate size (in.): 38 x 17 x 17 (each)
Materials: mahogany, copper, leather

500 N. Guadalupe St., Ste. G 932
Santa Fe, NM 87501
(505) 471-0534
FAX (505) 471-0534
hofferfurniture@hotmail.com

DESIGN CHARGES:	sketches free, cost of scaled drawings (rate varies) rolled into purchase price
DEPOSIT:	50% with balance due on completion
LEAD TIME:	2 months
LOCAL DELIVERY:	free
LONG DISTANCE:	air or surface freight, plus crating charge

Miles Clay Designs

"I feel grateful that I'm able to do something I love for my life's work, while at the same time improving the quality of my clients' lives."

ALTHOUGH MILES CLAY does build traditional types of furniture such as tables and desks, he specializes in custom-designed, one-of-a-kind, freestanding entertainment centers.

Three years of high school woodshop was Clay's only formal training in woodworking, but 18 years of professional experience has equipped him with the requisite technical knowledge. In addition, he has a degree in interior design from Woodbury University in Los Angeles. This degree and a strong interest in stereo and home-theater equipment have been essential aides in solving the design and engineering problems associated with the entertainment centers Clay builds.

He prefers to work with veneers because of the range of colors and figures available and the opportunity to create bookmatches and repeats across the surfaces of the finished work.

Clay's work has appeared in *Audio Video Interiors, Home Theater Interiors,* as well as in *Sunset, Home,* and *Los Angeles* magazines.

ENTERTAINMENT CENTER
Approximate size (in.): 120 x 204 x 30
Materials: maple, quilted maple, lacewood, ebony

ENTERTAINMENT CENTER
Approximate size (in.): 108 x 168 x 30
Materials: maple, bird's-eye maple,
brass, aluminum, mirrors

ENTERTAINMENT CENTER
Approximate size (in.): 90 x 192 x 30
Materials: maple, bird's-eye maple,
MDF, aluminum, copper

25815 Springbrook Ave.
Santa Clarita, CA 91350
(661) 255-9059
FAX (661) 259-9848
milesclay.designs@verizon.net

DESIGN CHARGES:	approximately 10% of budget, rolled into purchase price
DEPOSIT:	50% with balance paid in installments
LEAD TIME:	2–6 months
LOCAL DELIVERY:	inquire
LONG DISTANCE:	best available shipper, plus crating charge

Miters Touch

"I love the entire process: inspiration, design, woodworking, and the client's appreciation at the end. As a result, I have a very loyal client base."

DENISE GROHS is a rarity: a woman working in a field traditionally dominated by men. But Grohs' special status hasn't kept her from reaching her career goals. With the help of five employees, she runs a shop that has earned a regional reputation for excellence and versatility. Her shop is, in fact, the only one in her area producing art furniture as well as custom furniture and custom cabinetry, much of which exhibits her love of clean, contemporary mixes of two woods or of wood and another media.

Grohs makes most of her furniture from solid wood selected from hardwoods indigenous to her part of North Carolina: maple, cherry, walnut, ash, and oak. She assembles her work using traditional joinery and applies a variety of finishes.

Her work has appeared in juried shows throughout the Southeast.

ARMOIRE
Approximate size (in.): 80 x 48 x 22
Materials: maple, walnut

SCREEN

Approximate size (in.): 72 x 66 x 2
Materials: ash, mahogany, silk by
Laura Holshouser

DRESSER

Approximate size (in.): 36 x 40 x 20
Material: cherry

DETAIL

Denise Grohs
6858 Hwy. 105 S.
Boone, NC 28607
(828) 963-4445
FAX (828) 963-4488
miterstouch@boone.net
www.miterstouchinc.com

DESIGN CHARGES:	inquire
DEPOSIT:	30%–50% with additional payments as work progresses, final 10% due on completion
LEAD TIME:	3–6 months
LOCAL DELIVERY:	$20 per person per hour, plus gas
LONG DISTANCE:	commercial shipper, plus crating charge

Morton Fine Furniture, Inc.

"My aim is to retain the integrity of the furniture-making profession by crafting furniture that is both stylish and comfortable."

WITH THE HELP of four employees, Thomas Morton builds a line of furniture he describes as simple and timeless. Some pieces are inspired by the Pennsylvania Germans, who first settled Lancaster County. Others look to more recent models, specifically the Shakers and the cabinetmakers of the Arts and Crafts movement.

Morton uses only native American hardwoods, sometimes combining two woods in the same piece to create interesting contrasts. He assembles the furniture using traditional joinery and finishes it with natural oil and wax.

Morton's work has been featured in many regional publications as well as in *Woodshop News.* The quality of his work has been recognized by historical organizations in Pennsylvania: He has been commissioned to reproduce a series of candlesticks by the Ephrata Cloister and has done restoration work at Wheatland, the home of President James Buchanan.

CHEVAL MIRROR
Approximate size (in.): 72 x 31 x 16
Materials: cherry, tiger maple

DETAIL

TWELVE-DRAWER TALL CHEST
Approximate size (in.): 58 x 42 x 21
Materials: cherry, poplar

MORRIS CHAIR
Approximate size (in.): 40 x 35 x 40
Materials: tiger maple, leather

Thomas B. Morton
30 S. Hershey Ave.
Leola, PA 17540
(717) 656-3799, (877) 656-3799
FAX (717) 656-7179
mortontb@aol.com
www.mortonfinefurniture.com

DESIGN CHARGES:	$45 per hour, assessed only if the piece isn't purchased
DEPOSIT:	50% with balance due on completion
LEAD TIME:	4–6 months
LOCAL DELIVERY:	free in Lancaster County, $1.50 per mile outside of county
LONG DISTANCE:	worldwide shipping, plus crating charge

Timothy Mowry

"I don't have a line of furniture that I produce and sell. While I will reproduce an existing design if requested, I think, as many of my clients do, that it's far more exciting to forge ahead with each new piece."

TIMOTHY MOWRY has drawn inspiration from Craftsman and oriental originals, but the furniture that issues from his shop is distinctly his own. His work is identified by the use of details—curves, shadow lines, woven panels—that Mowry uses to invite the viewer to explore each piece more closely.

Mowry works primarily in solid wood assembled with traditional joinery. When he does apply veneers, he prefers to use veneers that he has cut. He uses hand-applied oil finishes, unless specifically requested to apply a spray finish.

He has shown his work at several East Coast venues, winning the title of Best New Artist in Wood Medium at the Philadelphia Furniture and Furnishings Show in 1999.

WALL CABINET
Approximate size (in.): 24 x 16 x 7
Materials: oak, spalted maple, ebony, reed

DINING TABLE
Approximate size (in.): 30 x 96 x 44
Materials: cherry, maple

WALL MIRROR
Approximate size (in.): 36 x 24 x 3
Materials: cocobolo, cherry,
   bird's-eye maple

BUFFET CABINET
Approximate size (in.): 33 x 50 x 20
Materials: cherry, curly cherry, maple, ebony

234 Severn Dr.
Annapolis, MD 21401
(410) 349-2929
tim@timothymowry.com
www.timothymowry.com

DESIGN CHARGES:	inquire
DEPOSIT:	33% with order, 33% when construction begins, with balance due on completion
LEAD TIME:	5–6 months
LOCAL DELIVERY:	$100
LONG DISTANCE:	door-to-door packing and shipping company

Nojo Design

"I was initially influenced by Asian art and architecture, and my work continues to explore the relationship between form and function and the incorporation of traditional form with contemporary design."

JO ROESSLER sees furniture making as a way to bridge the gap between functional and non-functional art. Unlike those disciplines that are more traditionally placed under the art umbrella (painting and sculpture, for instance), furniture making adds function to the complications of form.

When Roessler designs a cabinet or a table, he must do more than create a beautiful object; he must also produce an object that carries out its intended function. In addition, this dimension of practicality provides Roessler with a means to encourage interaction between the objects he creates and the people who live with those objects.

Roessler prepared for his career as a furniture maker by earning a B.F.A. at the Rhode Island School of Design, then moving onto the graduate furniture program at the University of Massachusetts.

His work has appeared in shows and galleries throughout the Northeast. It has also been the subject of articles in *Woodshop News* and *Crafts Report*.

VOLVO CABINET
Approximate size (in.): 67 x 23 x 47
Materials: ash, bird's-eye maple, ebony

SIDEBOARD
Approximate size (in.): 36 x 69 x 21
Materials: cherry, curly cherry, walnut

DINING TABLE
Approximate size (in.): 30 x 75 x 42
Materials: cherry, walnut

BEDSIDE TABLES
Approximate size (in.): 24 x 15 x 15 (each)
Materials: cherry, ebony

STANDING CABINET
Approximate size (in.): 48 x 15 x 15
Materials: cherry, maple, curly maple

Jo R. Roessler
84 Cottage Street
Easthampton, MA 01027
(413) 527-9663
nojo@javanet.com
www.nojodesign.com

DESIGN CHARGES:	none
DEPOSIT:	33% with balance due on completion
LEAD TIME:	2–2½ months
LOCAL DELIVERY:	free
LONG DISTANCE:	FOB, Easthampton, MA

Norris Woodworking

"We approach design with a passion and let exquisite details define our original furniture and architectural woodworking."

WORKING WITH 10 EMPLOYEES in their shop, Abbott Norris and Jon Roske produce one-of-a-kind furniture, each piece tailored to the individual needs of their clients. Details such as antiquing, inlaid woods, marquetry, and forged and hand-carved pulls set their pieces apart.

Norris and Roske pride themselves on their experience with many different furniture styles and technical approaches. This breadth of knowledge gives them flexibility in both the design and construction processes. Norris puts it this way: "Each design dictates the methods required, whether it be simple joinery or intricate attention to detail in a specialty finish. Each piece defines its own elements—sometimes solid wood, perhaps a common domestic species, and at other times a rare and beautiful exotic veneer."

Their work has appeared in many juried exhibitions in the Northwest and in both regional and national publications.

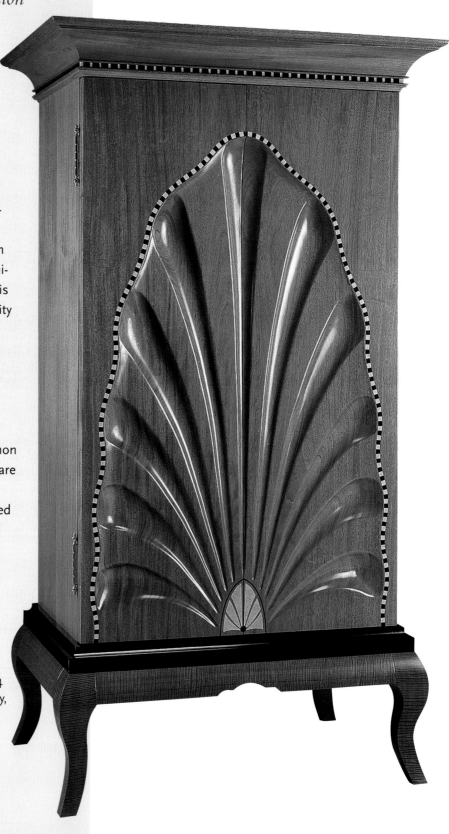

ARMOIRE
Approximate size (in.): 78 x 38 x 24
Materials: ebony, maple, mahogany, curly makore, cherry

BED
Approximate size (in.): 60 x 66 x 84
Material: mahogany

SOFA
Approximate size (in.): 60 x 84 x 32
Materials: lacewood, ebony, maple,
    brass, upholstery

TABLE
Approximate size (in.): 30 x 44 x 44
Materials: mahogany, curly maple, ebony

Abbott Norris, Jon Roske
313 N. First St.
Missoula, MT 59802-3625
(406) 721-2751
FAX (406) 721-1103
info@norriswoodworking.com
www.norriswoodworking.com

DESIGN CHARGES:	inquire
DEPOSIT:	33%–50% with balance due on completion
LEAD TIME:	2 months
LOCAL DELIVERY:	free
LONG DISTANCE:	best available shipper, plus crating charge

Peklo Design and Joinery

"Each piece is custom-designed to reflect my client's spirit and enhance his or her environment."

ANDREW PEKLO builds with wood and other natural materials such as leather, marble, glass, and brass because natural materials age well and are close to the human soul. This awareness of the spiritual content of fine furniture also impacts his design methods. He creates work that reflects not only his knowledge of good construction but also the spirit of each client.

Peklo combines his original designs with classical construction techniques. To this end, he works in solid wood using traditional joinery, completing each piece with a hand-rubbed finish.

His efforts have won Peklo recognition in shows throughout the state of Connecticut as well as in many neighboring states. His work has appeared on the pages of *Woodshop News*, *Home Furniture*, and several regional publications.

DESK
Approximate size (in.): 28 x 32 x 86
Materials: imbuia, leather, brass

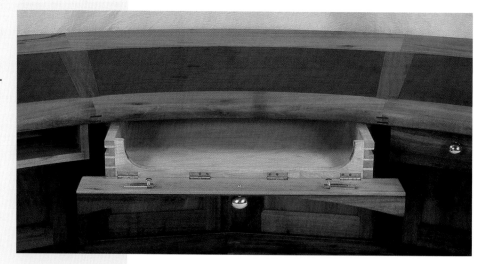

DETAIL

DINING CHAIR
Approximate size (in.): 56 x 26 x 24
Materials: imbuia, leather

DETAIL

JEWELRY BOX/TREASURE CHEST
Approximate size (in.): 72 x 20 x 19
Materials: curly maple, purpleheart

Andrew Peklo III
29 Pomperang Rd.
Woodbury, CT 06798
(203) 263-4566
FAX (203) 263-3951
themill@wtco.net
www.peklodesignandjoinery.com

DESIGN CHARGES:	approximately 10% of final cost
DEPOSIT:	33%–50% with balance due on completion
LEAD TIME:	inquire
LOCAL DELIVERY:	usually included
LONG DISTANCE:	best available shipper, plus crating charge

Peter Shepard Furniture

"My clients are drawn to my work for its uniqueness, proportion, and because it has tickled some aesthetic nerve for them."

PETER SHEPARD believes his clients are drawn to his work because it "tickles some aesthetic nerve." His work does so by exhibiting the three qualities that Shepard identifies in all successful furniture: It is visually appealing, functional, and well made.

Although Shepard builds furniture with specific historical antecedents (a bow-front chest of drawers or a chest on a stand, for instance), he gives this furniture a contemporary look through his experimentation with proportion, detailing, and wood selection. Notice, for example, the use of curly cherry and the ebony accents in the chest of drawers shown at right.

Shepard's work has appeared in juried exhibitions throughout the Northeast. His work has also appeared in *Fine Woodworking, Home Furniture, Woodshop News,* and *Design Book Seven* (The Taunton Press, 1996).

CHEST OF DRAWERS
Approximate size (in.): 43 x 35 x 21
Materials: curly cherry, ebony

STANDING DESK
Approximate size (in.): 42 x 29 x 24
Materials: white oak, ebony

TABLE
Approximate size (in.): 34 x 54 x 15
Materials: bubinga, ebony

HALL CHEST
Approximate size (in.): 34 x 27 x 18
Materials: curly maple, ebony

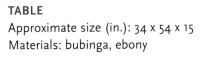

82 Littleton County Rd.
Harvard, MA 01451
(978) 456-9500
FAX (978) 456-8165

DESIGN CHARGES:	$300–$500, often rolled into purchase price
DEPOSIT:	10%; inquire about schedule for remaining payments
LEAD TIME:	12 months
LOCAL DELIVERY:	$200 or less
LONG DISTANCE:	best available shipper, plus crating charge of approximately $100

Dennis Paul Peterson

"Furniture should inspire. Are strength and beauty evident? If these exist, I have been successful in the making."

DENNIS PAUL PETERSON acknowledges the importance of beautiful material, solid construction, and sound technique in the creation of custom furniture. But these essential elements, he believes, must work hand in hand with a characteristic he identifies as the work's "design soul." This is a quality that reflects the stamp of the maker, as well as the beauty and proportion of the natural world.

Peterson believes this "design soul" can enable a piece of furniture to appeal to the beholder in much the same way as do the other visual arts, inspiring an emotional response in addition to an intellectual appreciation of the object's fitness for its purpose.

His work has won recognition in shows throughout Ohio, winning first place in 1999 for commercial furniture in the *Custom Woodworking Business* magazine portfolio awards.

COLLECTOR'S CASE
Approximate size (in.): 62 x 20 x 16
Materials: purpleheart, figured maple, ash, glass

CUPBOARD
Approximate size (in.): 72 x 18 x 18
Materials: curly maple, bubinga, maple

BENCH
Approximate size (in.): 36 x 60 x 18
Materials: oak, wenge

HALL TABLE
Approximate size (in.): 30 x 44 x 12
Materials: maple, figured cherry

P. O. Box 372
St. Marys, OH 45885
(419) 394-7305
FAX (419) 394-7305
dpp1@bright.net

DESIGN CHARGES:	$25 per hour, 50% rolled into purchase price
DEPOSIT:	50% with balance due on completion
LEAD TIME:	1½–3 months
LOCAL DELIVERY:	$15–$20
LONG DISTANCE:	best available shipper, plus crating charge

Peter S. Turner, Furnituremaker

"I use lightness and grace to express function and structural integrity."

THE GAMING TABLE shown on the facing page is an expression of Peter Turner's efforts to combine simplicity and visual interest in the same piece. The forms of the table and stools are straight-forward, but because they have been fashioned from bird's-eye maple, these simple forms present a surface that intrigues the eye.

Although he doesn't work in a particular style, Turner does acknowledge his debt to historical sources, particularly the furniture of the Shakers. Their influence is evident in the simplicity and directness of his designs, as well as the traditional solid-wood joinery he employs in construction.

Turner's work has appeared in many juried shows and exhibitions, including the Philadelphia Furniture and Furnishings Show every year since its inception. In addition, his work has appeared in a number of books and magazines.

ENTERTAINMENT CENTER
Approximate size (in.): 83 x 44 x 28
Materials: maple, ebony

DETAIL

GAMING TABLE
Approximate sizes (in.): 35 x 27 x 18 (table),
   25 x 12 (each stool)
Materials: bird's-eye maple, granadillo

SIDE CHAIR
Approximate size (in.): 38 x 20 x 17
Material: maple

126 Boothby Ave.
S. Portland, ME 04106
(207) 799-5503
FAX (207) 799-5503
petersturner@hotmail.com

DESIGN CHARGES:	$250 rolled into purchase price
DEPOSIT:	20% on signing, 30% at start of construction, with balance due on completion
LEAD TIME:	3–6 months
LOCAL DELIVERY:	inquire
LONG DISTANCE:	best available shipper, plus crating charge

Philip C. Lowe,
Maker of Fine Furniture

"My business provides a design service that can help people achieve a distinctive piece of furniture that can meet their needs not only in dimension but also in the type of wood and finish."

PHILIP LOWE acknowledges the influence of the classical masters of American furniture making. Even when creating a 20th-century piece like the entertainment center shown on the facing page, Lowe incorporates the design sensibilities of those masters to create a form that is solidly based on a historical foundation.

Lowe constructs his furniture from solid wood using mortise-and-tenon and dovetail joinery. He also makes use of exotic species and figures by slicing those materials into veneers. His finishes are hand-applied, then rubbed out to maximum smoothness.

Lowe's work is in the permanent collection of a number of national historic sites, including President Lincoln's home and Ellis Island. He has also written extensively in the woodworking press and has made several videos on high-style furniture reproduction. In addition, he has served as head instructor at the North Bennet Street School in Boston.

DETAIL

DESK WITH SECRETARY
Approximate size (in.): 96 x 45 x 22
Materials: walnut, pine

ENTERTAINMENT CENTER
Approximate size (in.): 84 x 30 x 26
Materials: mahogany, oak

CARVED SHERATON BED
Approximate size (in.): 96 x 53 x 75
Materials: mahogany, pine, maple

DETAIL

116 Water St.
Beverly, MA 01915
(978) 922-0615
FAX (978) 922-0615
furnitur@shore.net
www.furnituremakingclasses.com

DESIGN CHARGES:	inquire
DEPOSIT:	50% with balance due on completion
LEAD TIME:	inquire
LOCAL DELIVERY:	inquire
LONG DISTANCE:	best available shipper, plus crating charge

185

Peter Robert Presnell

*"My goal is to present a finished piece
of work that will fit as well 50 years from
now as it does at this moment."*

PETER PRESNELL acknowledges his debt to turn-of-the-century designers/craftsmen like Stickley, William Morris, and Greene and Greene. But although his work is rooted in that rich soil, Presnell has created his own style, which he refers to as High Western Deco.

He seeks to design pieces with presence rather than ego; in other words, furniture that can coexist peacefully with other furnishings in clients' homes, standing shoulder to shoulder with those furnishings without evoking a spirit of competition.

Presnell's approach to the engineering of his work follows traditional models. He favors mortise-and-tenon joinery for his casework, frame-and-panel door construction, and dovetails at the front and back of each drawer. When faced with a construction problem, he searches for what he identifies as the "elegant solution."

His work has won him Best of Show recognition at exhibitions at The College of the Redwoods and at the Ambiance Gallery in Eureka, California. His work has also appeared in several publications, including *Fine Woodworking*.

SIDE CHAIR
Approximate size (in.): 40 x 18 x 21
Materials: cherry, rosewood

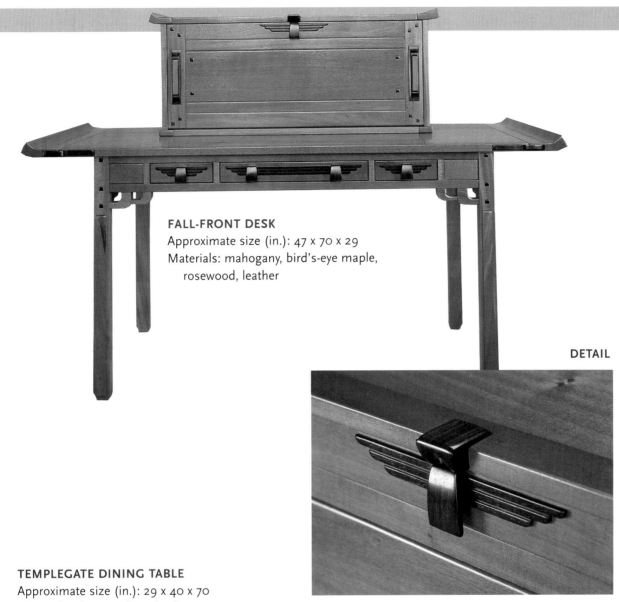

FALL-FRONT DESK
Approximate size (in.): 47 x 70 x 29
Materials: mahogany, bird's-eye maple,
    rosewood, leather

DETAIL

TEMPLEGATE DINING TABLE
Approximate size (in.): 29 x 40 x 70
Materials: cherry, walnut, bird's-eye
    maple, curly maple

3177 Greenwood Heights Dr.
Kneeland, CA 95549
(707) 442-6532
rainmakr@humboldt1.com

DESIGN CHARGES:	no charge if client has made a deposit on the finished piece
DEPOSIT:	50% with balance due on completion
LEAD TIME:	2–6 months
LOCAL DELIVERY:	free
LONG DISTANCE:	best available shipper, plus crating charge

Randy Weersing Furniture Design and Fabrication

"Mine is a small, one-person operation stressing integrity of design and construction."

BECAUSE RANDY WEERSING works alone, his furniture possesses "a continuity and clarity of vision." In this shop, what the designer conceives the designer also executes. Weersing believes that his one-man-band approach offers his clients the best possible opportunity to have their individual visions realized because a client who speaks to Weersing is speaking simultaneously to the designer and to the craftsman.

Weersing prefers to use "nonthreatened" wood species in his work. He assembles that work using traditional joinery, although he will use contemporary joinery and materials where such options are preferable. In particular, he favors mortise-and-tenon and dovetail construction.

Weersing has exhibited on the West Coast, most notably in several juried shows at the Maude Kearns Gallery. His work has also been featured in local newspapers and in the *Better Homes and Gardens* "Building Ideas" issue.

COFFEE TABLE
Approximate size (in.): 18 x 36 x 36
Material: white oak

SHOE CHEST
Approximate size (in.): 21 x 54 x 17
Materials: cherry, maple, ash

DESK
Approximate size (in.): 46 x 54 x 36
Materials: cherry, ebony, copper, leaded glass

TEA TABLE
Approximate size (in.): 20 x 48 x 27
Materials: walnut, ebony

24865 Fir Grove Ln.
Elmira, OR 97437
(541) 935-2486
FAX (541) 935-1638
rweersing@aol.com
www.member.aol.com/rweersing

DESIGN CHARGES:	inquire
DEPOSIT:	33% with balance due on completion
LEAD TIME:	6 months
LOCAL DELIVERY:	free within 30 miles
LONG DISTANCE:	best available shipper, plus crating charge

Rasche Cabinetmakers

"Flights of design fancy are never allowed to compromise structure and function."

J. MARK RASCHE is a traditionalist. Although his work is often put to modern uses (housing audio and video equipment, for example), it is furniture thoroughly secured to its period roots. In large part, this reflects Rasche's personal preferences, but it also reflects the preferences of his customers, many of whom come to him initially for antique restoration.

Rasche uses a mix of hand- and power-tool operations in the construction of his furniture. The use of power tools is an acknowledgment of the realities of a modern cabinetmaking shop in which construction must occur at a certain pace. The use of hand tools is a manifestation of Rasche's belief that any cabinetmaker worth his salt should know how to hand-cut dovetails.

Rasche's work has appeared in *Columbus Monthly* magazine and on local television.

DETAIL

CLOCK
Approximate size (in.):
84 x 21 x 11
Materials: cherry,
curly maple

HARVEST TABLE
Approximate size (in.):
29 x 76 x 44
Material: cherry

CHINESE MOON-GAZING CHAIR
Approximate size (in.): 35 x 27 x 31
Material: cherry

Sue and J. Mark Rasche
6962 Harlem Rd.
Westerville, OH 43082
(614) 882-1810
FAX (614) 882-1810
RascheCabinetmakers@juno.com

DESIGN CHARGES:	$250 rolled into purchase price
DEPOSIT:	50% with balance due on completion
LEAD TIME:	3–6 months
LOCAL DELIVERY:	free
LONG DISTANCE:	inquire

Owen Rein

"I work alone with a few simple hand tools and gather my own wood."

OWEN REIN'S approach to his craft clearly reflects the American tradition of country chairmaking. He begins work by hand-selecting the trees he will harvest. Then after the tree has been laid on the ground and sectioned, he splits the chair parts and shapes them using shaving tools, working largely by eye. For Rein, there are many advantages to this type of construction. "Chairs made this way are very strong because this technique considers many aspects of the internal structure of the wood," he says. "Plus, it produces work with an aesthetic quality that cannot be reproduced by modern methods."

Although he has studied with Ian Kirby, W. E. Strong, and Wheymond Evans, Rein is mostly self-taught, relying on experimentation and experience to guide him through the chairmaking process.

His chairs have appeared in many books and magazines, among them *Woodwork, Popular Woodworking,* and *American Woodworker.* He has also been the recipient of several prestigious commissions, having been called upon to build rocking chairs for U.S. Senator Dale Bumpers and former U.S. President Bill Clinton.

ROCKING CHAIR
Approximate size (in.): 48 x 25 x 34
Materials: oak, hickory, walnut, hickory bark

DETAIL

KITCHEN STOOL
Approximate size (in.): 29 x 15 x 15
Materials: oak, hickory bark

LOW-BACK WORK STOOL
Approximate size (in.): 34 x 18 x 15
Materials: hickory, ebony, hickory bark

DINING CHAIR
Approximate size (in.): 42 x 20 x 17
Materials: oak, hickory bark

P. O. Box 1162
Mountain View, AR 72560
(870) 269-5381
owenrein@hotmail.com
www.owenrein.com

DESIGN CHARGES: inquire
DEPOSIT: 20% with balance due on completion
LEAD TIME: 3–6 months
LOCAL DELIVERY: free
LONG DISTANCE: inquire

Riverside Artisans, Inc.

"I make every effort to reach a design that best fulfills the demands of the piece and the client's wishes."

DURING HIS APPRENTICESHIP, Jim Galileo had the opportunity to work in many different furniture styles and periods. This historical foundation allows him to incorporate elements of classic period furniture into the contemporary work he now produces.

His work features what he describes as "interrupted curves," a design characteristic that requires the use of bent laminations as well as veneering on curved panels. Variations of these curves can be seen in the pieces shown on these pages.

Galileo is unstinting in the close, personal attention he gives his clients during the design process, and he believes this attention, along with the quality of execution exhibited by his work, is what keeps his clients happy.

LINEN CHEST
Approximate size (in.): 18 x 34 x 15
Material: pine

HALL TABLE
Approximate size (in.): 34 x 54 x 15
Materials: mahogany, pomelle
  sapele

ENTERTAINMENT CENTER
Approximate size (in.): 84 x 120 x 34
Materials: curly maple, pearwood

DETAIL

Jim Galileo
1 Mountainside Rd.
Warwick, NY 10990
(973) 278-5881
FAX (845) 258-9043

DESIGN CHARGES:	$75 per hour rolled into purchase price
DEPOSIT:	50% with balance due on delivery
LEAD TIME:	4 months
LOCAL DELIVERY:	free
LONG DISTANCE:	best available shipper, plus 2%–5% crating charge

Robert Brown Design

"Using a variety of materials, I have attempted to design objects resulting in an environment or atmosphere that relates metaphorically or conceptually to the function of the object."

ROBERT H. BROWN brings a background in anthropology to the practice of furniture making. At first glance, this may seem an unlikely marriage of interests, but it makes perfect sense to Brown. Both anthropology and furniture making are intimately involved with the icons of human culture: Furniture makers create icons, and anthropologists study them.

Brown's preparation for his career reflects these two interests. Seventeen years after he received his B.A. in anthropology from the University of California, he received his M.F.A. in furniture design from San Diego State University. In between, Brown sandwiched a wood technology certificate from Laney College and an apprenticeship with Art Carpenter.

Brown's work has been featured in several magazines, and he has exhibited throughout California.

ORIGAMI CHAIR
Approximate size (in.): 33 x 16 x 16
Materials: plywood, ebony

COMPOUND MITERED TRESTLE TABLE
Approximate size (in.): 29 x 78 x 36
Materials: walnut, marble

DETAIL

DINING TABLE
Approximate size (in.): 29 x 78 x 32
Material: white oak

7871 Quince St.
La Mesa, CA 91941
(619) 460-6026
FAX (619) 460-6026
robert-brown-design@home.com
www.robert-brown-design.com

DESIGN CHARGES:	$30 per hour not rolled into purchase price
DEPOSIT:	60% with balance due on completion
LEAD TIME:	6 months
LOCAL DELIVERY:	inquire
LONG DISTANCE:	blanket-wrap shipper, plus crating charge

Robert Erickson Woodworking

"A well-conceived wooden chair will fill the imagination. It must delight from different views. It should be ceremonial yet familiar. Ultimately, it should know how you like to sit."

ROBERT ERICKSON likes a challenge. He is drawn to chairmaking because of the difficulties inherent in creating furniture capable of accommodating the human body, while at the same time discovering "freshness of shape and line in something so familiar to every living space." He is similarly drawn to the creative challenge of running a business that is flexible enough to respond to the needs of a varied clientele but at the same time successful enough to support his family and those of his three employees.

In his 30 years as a furniture maker, Erickson has exhibited in juried shows across the country. He has been the subject of one-man shows at galleries and museums in Norway, Nebraska, New Mexico, and California. Examples of his work have been added to the collections of the Yale University Art Gallery, Los Angeles County Museum of Art, Minnesota Museum of Art, and Renwick Gallery, Smithsonian American Art Museum.

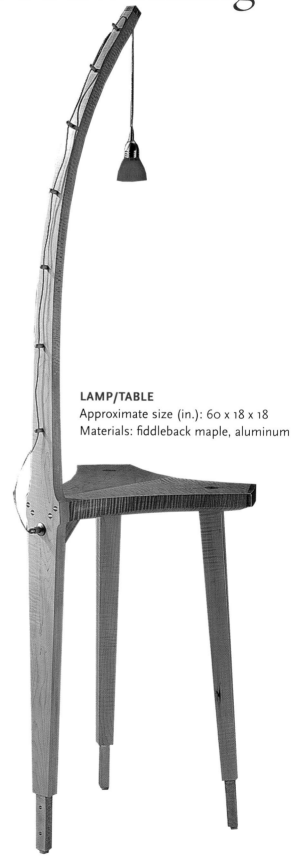

LAMP/TABLE
Approximate size (in.): 60 x 18 x 18
Materials: fiddleback maple, aluminum

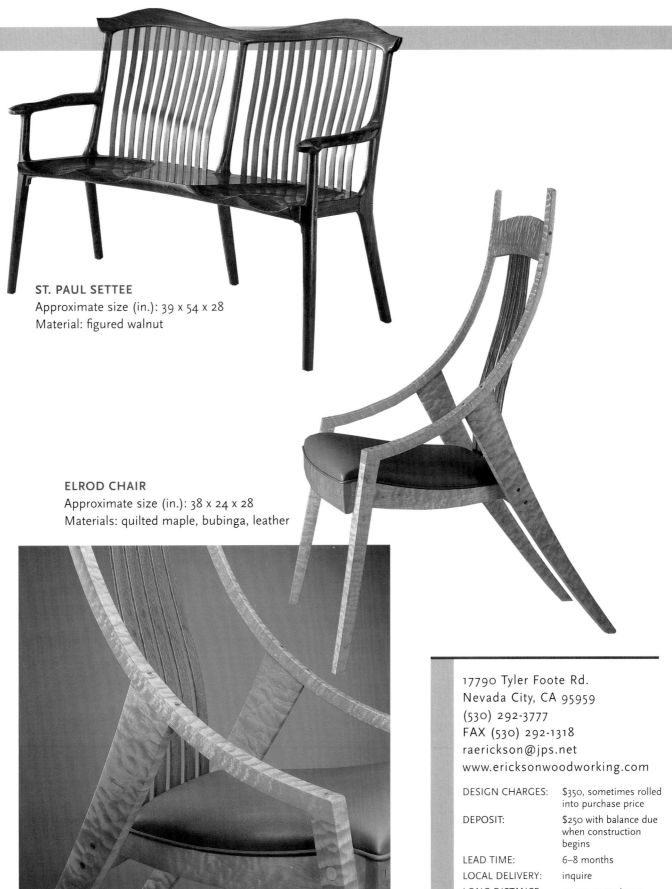

ST. PAUL SETTEE
Approximate size (in.): 39 x 54 x 28
Material: figured walnut

ELROD CHAIR
Approximate size (in.): 38 x 24 x 28
Materials: quilted maple, bubinga, leather

DETAIL

17790 Tyler Foote Rd.
Nevada City, CA 95959
(530) 292-3777
FAX (530) 292-1318
raerickson@jps.net
www.ericksonwoodworking.com

DESIGN CHARGES:	$350, sometimes rolled into purchase price
DEPOSIT:	$250 with balance due when construction begins
LEAD TIME:	6–8 months
LOCAL DELIVERY:	inquire
LONG DISTANCE:	common carrier or blanket-wrap shipper, plus crating charge

Ron Day Designs

"Clients usually come to me because they haven't found what they want in show-rooms, catalogs, or other media. We work together in the design process, a close relationship in which I guide and suggest, to give form to the clients' ideas."

RON DAY builds exclusively on commission, working with his clients to create furniture that is not only utilitarian but also displays "clean lines, harmonious proportions, subtle detailing, and the beauty of natural wood." A background in art and furniture repair has aided him in the resolution of design problems brought to him by his clients.

Day enjoys creating pieces that reveal the natural color, grain, and texture of wood. He typically chooses domestic hardwoods but does occasionally work with exotic species, most commonly ebony. He employs traditional joinery, relying on the strength of mortise-and-tenon and dovetail construction.

His work has appeared in a number of national magazines, including *House Beautiful, Fine Homebuilding, Home Furniture,* and *Wood Digest.*

COFFEE TABLE
Approximate size (in.): 17 x 42 x 20
Materials: mahogany, California walnut, ebony inlay

DETAIL

DINING TABLE
Approximate size (in.): 31 x 90 x 42
Materials: flame birch, bird's-eye maple,
ebony inlay

DINING TABLE
Approximate size (in.): 30 x 72 x 48
Materials: California walnut, ebony
inlay

1801 17th Ave.
Santa Cruz, CA 95062
(831) 477-0911
FAX (831) 477-0911
ronday@cruzio.com
www.loon.com/RonDayDesigns

DESIGN CHARGES:	$300 rolled into purchase price
DEPOSIT:	33% with balance due on completion
LEAD TIME:	3 months
LOCAL DELIVERY:	$25
LONG DISTANCE:	freight company, plus crating charge

Sammis Woodworking

"Working one on one with the customer throughout the design process allows me to create one-of-a-kind pieces of quality."

JON SAMMIS didn't start out to be a maker of custom furniture. Initially he was a cabinetmaker who created one-of-a-kind work for his family in his spare time, but soon a clientele noticed his furniture and began placing orders.

Sammis prefers using a combination of exotic veneers and solid wood, although he does sometimes turn to domestic species such as curly cherry and walnut. He assembles his work using a wide range of traditional joinery, including splined miters, mortises and tenons, and dovetails.

He encourages buyers of custom furniture to keep records of the features they would like to see in the furniture they'll order. Those records might take the form of magazine clippings or sketches or verbal descriptions. "Then when the time comes we can pick and choose the details to design your ultimate custom piece."

HUTCH
Approximate size (in.): 84 x 60 x 16
Materials: Japanese Tamo ash,
European oak, African wenge

SIDEBOARD
Approximate size (in.): 34 x 60 x 16
Materials: ash, oak, wenge

COFFEE TABLE
Approximate size (in.): 18 x 36 x 48
Materials: quilted pomelle sapele,
African wenge, mahogany

CEDAR CHEST
Approximate size (in.): 18 x 36 x 18
Material: Figured bird's-eye maple,
curly maple

Jon Sammis
P. O. Box 115
Petersham, MA 01366
(978) 724-6608

DESIGN CHARGES:	$75 per hour rolled into purchase price
DEPOSIT:	50% with balance due on completion
LEAD TIME:	1–3 months
LOCAL DELIVERY:	inquire
LONG DISTANCE:	independent trucking company, plus crating charge

Scott Ernst Custom Woodworks

"I design and craft furniture to specifically meet the needs of my client's personality, aesthetic, and space."

SCOTT ERNST works with what he calls "domestic exotic" wood: curly, spalted, wormy. These materials give the surfaces of his furniture an energy unlike the surfaces of furniture built with more sedately figured material.

Ernst believes that fine craftwork can't be fully appreciated at first glance, that it must be experienced over time. He therefore strives to include details that may not be evident on the day a client takes possession of a piece of furniture. The furniture has details "you may not notice until your hand falls on them or the sun travels enough to allow a hard edge to reveal a shadow in the midst of a soft curve."

DETAIL

COMPUTER DESK AND CHAIR
Approximate sizes (in.): 30 x 53 x 24 (desk), 41 x 19 x 19 (chair)
Materials: wormy figured maple, African blackwood

SIDEBOARD
Approximate size (in.): 36 x 56 x 20
Material: curly maple

TABLE
Approximate size (in.): 30 x 60 x 30
Material: cherry

HC 70, Box 9B
Glorieta, NM 87535
(505) 757-2786
(877) 401-1287
FAX (877) 401-1287
www.scott.ernst.org

DESIGN CHARGES:	$40 per hour not rolled into purchase price
DEPOSIT:	40% with balance due on completion
LEAD TIME:	2–6 months
LOCAL DELIVERY:	free
LONG DISTANCE:	freight company, plus crating charge

Signature Gallery

"The bulk of our business is audio/video related. We know how to make it all work."

A FURNITURE MAKER who specializes in audio/video cabinetry, Edward Schoen is equipped to handle the particular problems this work can sometimes pose.

He works in a variety of styles, ranging from 18th-century-inspired country cabinetry to sleek contemporary work. This versatility is a result of his long and varied experience as a woodworker, which began at Bucks County Community College. He then attended the College of the Redwoods in the program's first year. Interspersed with this formal training was a series of jobs in California cabinet shops.

Schoen has exhibited in several California venues over the last 20 years, as well as in the Philadelphia Furniture and Furnishings Show the last five years. He has also contributed to *Audio Video Interiors* and *American Woodworker* magazines.

COMPACT DISC CABINET
Approximate size (in.): 60 x 36 x 16
Material: tiger maple

ENTERTAINMENT CABINET
Approximate size (in.): 90 x 76 x 24
Materials: bird's-eye maple, rosewood, ebony

CABINET
Approximate size (in.): 104 x 144 x 30
Materials: bird's-eye maple, tiger
    maple, ebony, wenge

TELEVISION CABINET
Approximate size (in.): 52 x 46 x 23
Materials: purpleheart, ash

Edward and Sherrie Schoen
4020 Skippack Pike
P. O. Box 11
Skippack, PA 19474
(610) 584-9022
FAX (610) 584-9424
siggal@enter.net
www.signaturegalleryfurniture.com

DESIGN CHARGES:	none
DEPOSIT:	33% with balance due on completion
LEAD TIME:	3–4 months
LOCAL DELIVERY:	free
LONG DISTANCE:	blanket-wrap shipper, plus crating charge

Skantyllion

"I find the doing the most fulfilling, and the little discoveries and the challenge of instructing others keep me energized."

LARRY FAGAN made the change from aerospace design (hydraulic flight-control actuators) to fine furniture making thanks to a series of classes he took with James Krenov, lead instructor of the College of the Redwoods. Fagan identifies Krenov's influence as the most potent in both his approach to design and his approach to shop practices.

Working alone, Fagan carefully constructs his designs from a combination of solid wood and resawn veneers, using traditional hand-cut joinery and a full range of classical techniques, such as coopering, bent laminating, carving, and marquetry. He often completes his pieces with hardware hand-made from wood or silver.

Fagan's work has appeared in The Taunton Press' *Design Book Seven*, in *American Woodworker* magazine, and in a number of regional publications. He is currently represented by Arts Prescott in Prescott, Arizona.

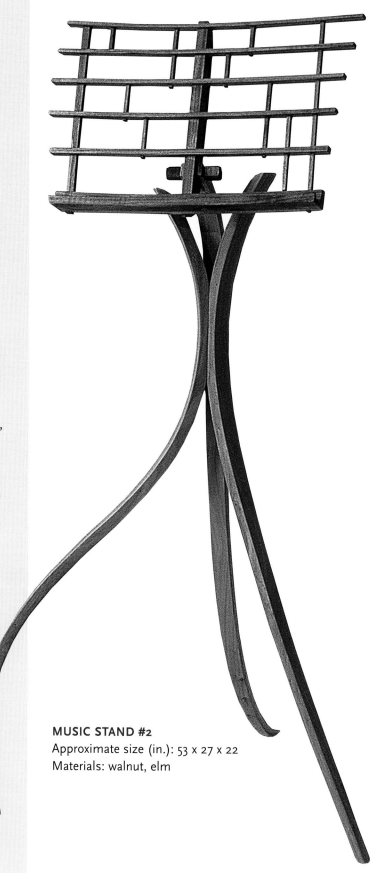

MUSIC STAND #2
Approximate size (in.): 53 x 27 x 22
Materials: walnut, elm

SIDEBOARD
Approximate size (in.): 36 x 60 x 13
Materials: koa, gonçalo alves, desert
  ironwood, oak

DETAIL

END TABLES
Approximate size (in.): 22 x 23 x 13 (each)
Materials: ash, juniper, silver

Larry Fagan
2315 Oakwood Dr.
Prescott, AZ 86305
(928) 776-1526
dlpf@computerlink.com

DESIGN CHARGES:	none
DEPOSIT:	50% with balance due on completion
LEAD TIME:	inquire
LOCAL DELIVERY:	free
LONG DISTANCE:	best available shipper, plus $50–$100 crating charge

Janice Smith

"Much of the furniture we live with is designed with only the front view in mind even though the entire mass impacts the space it occupies. It is important to me to design pieces as three-dimensional sculptural forms that engage the viewer from all angles."

JANICE SMITH believes that furniture must be functional, but she also believes it can "excite the viewer while fulfilling the function." To that end, she designs pieces that integrate function into a design often made up of sweeping curves and angles, unlike the forms more traditionally identified with furniture. Currently she's focusing on veneered plywood constructions (see the chairs in the photos on the facing page) because this material is well suited to the creation of those sweeping curves and angles.

In addition to her work as a furniture maker, Smith is currently teaching at Bucks County Community College, Moore College of Art and Design, and Drexel University. She previously taught at the University of Kansas and the Rhode Island School of Design. Her work has appeared in many galleries and exhibitions across the country.

WALL-HUNG TABLE
Approximate size (in.): 15 x 37 x 12
Material: cherry

CATHY LYNN KNOCK-DOWN CHAIR
Approximate size (in.): 30 x 29 x 32
Materials: cherry, plywood, upholstery

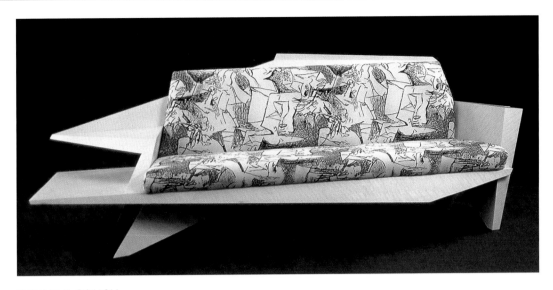

ORIGAMI COUCH
Approximate size (in.): 31 x 98 x 33
Materials: birch, plywood, veneer, upholstery

WHIMCYCLE CHAIR
Approximate size (in.): 31 x 53 x 27
Materials: plywood, veneer, steel
tubing, rubber wheels, upholstery

LATEEN CHAIR
Approximate size (in.):
38 x 66 x 24
Materials: plywood,
veneer, upholstery

715 S. 7th St.
Philadelphia, PA 19147
(215) 923-1447
not2wooden@@earthlink.net

DESIGN CHARGES:	$25 per hour or $300 rolled into purchase price
DEPOSIT:	50% with balance due on delivery
LEAD TIME:	2 months
LOCAL DELIVERY:	$25 per hour
LONG DISTANCE:	best available shipper, plus crating charge

Solomon Ross Furniture

"I simply aim to produce furniture that is soundly functional, sensuously beautiful, and built to endure."

Ross S. Peterson embraces the role of function in the furniture he designs and builds, striving "to express beauty in a utilitarian form."

The key to his success is his talent for visualizing the needs and desires of his clients. This, coupled with a conscious effort to keep those clients informed at every step in the design and construction process, has permitted Peterson to quickly build up his four-year-old business.

His work has won recognition (including two best-of-show awards) at each of the last five Northern Woods Exhibitions. In addition, he was designated the Best New Artist in Wood at the 1998 Philadelphia Furniture and Furnishings Show. His work has also appeared on the pages of *Woodshop News, Woodwork, American Woodworker,* and *Workbench* magazines.

DEMILUNE TABLE
Approximate size (in.):
    32 x 32 x 12
Materials: black acacia, cherry

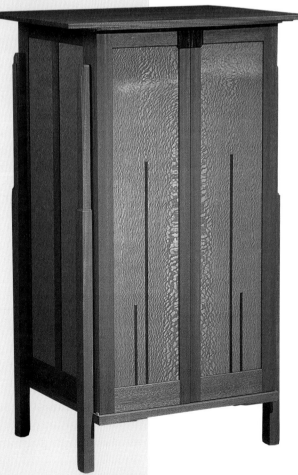

STEREO CABINET
Approximate size (in.): 44 x 28 x 20
Materials: lacewood, mahogany,
    cocobolo

SIDEBOARD
Approximate size (in.): 30 x 52 x 17
Materials: cherry, hophornbeam

DETAIL

BENCH
Approximate size (in.): 17 x 62 x 14
Material: ash

Ross S. Peterson
12066 Whitetail Ln.
Hanover, MN 55341
(763) 498-7911

DESIGN CHARGES:	10% of estimated final cost rolled into purchase price
DEPOSIT:	10% at signing, 50% at start of work, with balance due on completion
LEAD TIME:	9–12 months
LOCAL DELIVERY:	inquire
LONG DISTANCE:	blanket-wrap carrier, plus time-and-material crating charge

Stanton Hill Studios

"My personal style is contemporary, although it draws from traditional furniture styles so it works equally well in both modern and traditional decors."

T. BENJAMIN HOBBS believes buyers are drawn to his furniture because of the distinctive angular nature of his designs and because of the wood combinations he features that often highlight the natural beauty of domestic hardwoods. He assembles his furniture using traditional joinery and hand-finishes his pieces.

Hobbs identifies several stylistic influences: Arts and Crafts, oriental, and Art Deco. In his shop, these styles are combined in work that is not only functional but also artfully designed and expertly crafted.

Hobbs trained at the Rochester Institute of Technology, where he earned a B.A. specializing in woodworking and furniture design. Since his graduation, he has exhibited his work in many galleries and exhibitions throughout the United States.

CABINET
Approximate size (in.): 38 x 37 x 20
Material: cherry

DINING CHAIR
Approximate size (in.): 41 x 18 x 24
Materials: cherry, walnut, upholstery

TRESTLE HALL TABLE
Approximate size (in.): 32 x 48 x 14
Materials: cherry, walnut

SUNBURST LAMP
Approximate size (in.): 71 x 17 x 17
Materials: maple, cherry, tiger maple, copper

T. Benjamin Hobbs
2320 Stanton Hill
Nichols, NY 13812
(607) 687-3459
stantstu@pronetisp.net

DESIGN CHARGES:	$200 rolled into purchase price
DEPOSIT:	33%–50% with balance due on completion
LEAD TIME:	2–12 months
LOCAL DELIVERY:	inquire
LONG DISTANCE:	best available shipper, plus crating charge

Stephen H. Smith, Cabinetmaker

"I enjoy the design aspect of my work and, when possible, design my own interpretations of period styles."

STEPHEN SMITH believes his attention to hand-craftsmanship sets his work apart. He fashions every carved detail by hand. His moldings are created using handplanes. The final surfaces on his work are produced through hand-scraping and hand-sanding. This approach to woodworking produces textures that can't be matched by craftsmen who use only machine processes.

Smith builds his furniture with solid wood, using the same species employed by the original makers of New England period furniture: cherry, walnut, mahogany, and figured maple. Like those 18th- and 19th-century craftsmen, he relies on dovetail and mortise-and-tenon joinery to give his furniture strength.

Smith encourages his customers to involve themselves in the design process. This involvement, he believes, is the primary reason buyers are drawn to makers of custom furniture. "This is one of the most exciting aspects of having something built, feeling that you were part of the design process," he says.

SLANT-LID DESK
Approximate size (in.): 42 x 39 x 19
Materials: tiger maple, pine

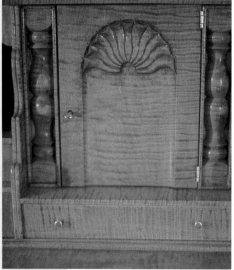

DETAIL

TEA TABLE
Approximate size (in.): 27 x 28 x 20
Material: curly maple

ARMCHAIR
Approximate size (in.):
42 x 22 x 20
Materials: cherry, poplar

9 Old Post Rd.
Clinton, CT 06413
(860) 669-9172
FAX (860) 669-9172
ctfurnituremaker@msn.com
www.ctfurnituremaker.com

DESIGN CHARGES:	none
DEPOSIT:	33% with balance due on delivery
LEAD TIME:	6–9 months
LOCAL DELIVERY:	free within 150 miles
LONG DISTANCE:	best available shipper, plus crating charge

Stephen Perrin Woodworking

"Born on paper, my designs in wood evolve to maturity in the making."

STEPHEN PERRIN begins work on a piece of furniture with a plan sketched on paper, but he allows the design to evolve during the construction process. He likes to keep himself open to the possibility that something unexpected might happen, some little twist to the original idea that more fully expresses what is essential about that particular piece of furniture.

Although his career as a professional furniture maker covers just 10 years, Perrin's work has been accepted by many juried exhibitions in venues all across the country, including by the American Craft Museum in New York. In addition, his work has appeared in many woodworking magazines, *The Washington Post,* and *The New York Times.* His work is also exhibited at the White House.

DROP-LEAF CORNER TABLE
Approximate size (in.): 32 x 33 x 21
Materials: tiger maple, bubinga

COFFEE TABLE
Approximate size (in.): 17 x 40 x 30
Material: cherry

BUFFET
Approximate size (in.): 34 x 72 x 20
Materials: tiger maple, cherry, wenge

SOFA TABLE
Approximate size (in.): 30 x 52 x 15
Materials: cherry, wenge, bird's-eye
   maple

330 W. 23rd St.
Baltimore, MD 21211
(410) 467-1290
FAX (410) 467-3929
perrinart@erols
www.guild.com

DESIGN CHARGES:	5% rolled into purchase price
DEPOSIT:	50% with balance due on completion
LEAD TIME:	2–3 months
LOCAL DELIVERY:	free
LONG DISTANCE:	best available shipper, plus crating charge

Craig Vandall Stevens

"Patience, personal commitment, and working at this level of refinement have helped me to become my own teacher and to find my own voice."

CRAIG VANDALL STEVENS strives to create work that is, in his words, "aesthetically pleasing, while adhering to my artistic values, attention to detail, and sense of quality." He works closely with his clients to develop original designs and concentrates on only one piece at a time. This approach reflects the instruction of Stevens's teacher, James Krenov, the lead instructor of The College of the Redwoods.

Working alone, Stevens produces his furniture from resawn veneers and air-dried solid wood using traditional joinery. He favors unusual, underused species, particularly those taken from tree farms practicing sustainable harvests.

Stevens's work has been the subject of many articles in both the mainstream and woodworking press. In addition, he is the author of several woodworking books and several articles for *Fine Woodworking* magazine.

DETAIL

DAME GRANADILLO
Approximate size (in.): 50 x 25 x 14
Materials: granadillo, fiddleback maple, spalted maple, spalted swiss pear, bubinga, brass

GINKGO VITRINE
Approximate size (in.): 63 x 27 x 12
Materials: narra, wenge, chechen, satinwood, English walnut, cuta, arrariba

MAPLE DINING CHAIR
Approximate size (in.): 40 x 18 x 18
Materials: maple, fiddleback maple, upholstery

11951 Wildwood Ln.
Sunbury, OH 43074
(740) 965-8049
cvstevens@mindspring.com
www.cvstevens.com

DESIGN CHARGES:	none
DEPOSIT:	33% with balance due on completion
LEAD TIME:	2–4 months
LOCAL DELIVERY:	free
LONG DISTANCE:	air freight, plus crating charge

Stevenson Classic Woodworking

"My work expresses my yearning to be back in the 18th century."

ROBERT G. STEVENSON doesn't want to just build in the manner of his 18th-century predecessors, he wants to actually live in that period. This desire was inspired by a childhood spent on the North Shore of Massachusetts surrounded by beautiful antique furniture. Later, his interest in 18th-century life and work was reignited when he inherited a collection of hand tools from his great-uncle and his great-grandfather. After Stevenson retired from the navy, it was logical for him to put these tools to work in the reproduction of classic furniture.

Working alone, he produces a line of reproduction furniture firmly rooted in 18th-century New England. To make his work as faithful as possible to the originals, Stevenson has wood shipped to his California shop from New England. He also stays true to 18th-century construction methods by using mostly hand techniques and animal hide glue.

Stevenson's work has won many awards at the Design in Wood Show in San Diego. His work has also appeared in *Woodwork* magazine, *Woodshop News,* and *Early American Homes,* which identified Stevenson as one of the 200 best craftsmen in America.

FEDERAL-PERIOD GAME TABLE
Approximate size (in.): 30 x 36 x 18 (36 when open)
Materials: mahogany, primavera, satinwood, ebony, holly, pine

DETAIL

SIDEBOARD
Approximate size (in.): 32 x 62 x 21
Materials: cherry, mahogany, bird's-eye maple,
satinwood, ebony, vegetable ivory

TALL CLOCK
Approximate size (in.): 93 x 22 x 12
Materials: mahogany, pine, mixed
woods, brass

Robert G. Stevenson Jr.
662 Guava Ave.
Chula Vista, CA 91910-5441
(619) 422-7338
FAX (619) 422-7338
bobscww@cs.com

DESIGN CHARGES:	$30 per hour rolled into purchase price
DEPOSIT:	50% with balance due on completion
LEAD TIME:	1½–3 months
LOCAL DELIVERY:	free
LONG DISTANCE:	inquire

The Studio of Andrew Millican

"Decorative arts have the ability to bring day-to-day objects to the level of the fine arts, not in the grand scale of things but in the human scale."

ANDREW MILLICAN'S goal is to create "eloquent objects," objects that tell a tale, either personal or public. To achieve this, Millican searches for insights into the lives of his clients that will permit him to develop "symbolism central to that client's relationships or milestones." His use of marquetry and inlay in wood, stone, and metal provides him with a visual language through which he can express this symbolism.

After completing his training at the North Bennet Street School in Boston, Millican continued his woodworking education by working for six years in the shops of other furniture makers. In 1990 he opened his own shop, where he usually works alone.

Millican's work has appeared in juried exhibitions throughout Massachusetts as well as in New York City.

DINING CHAIR
Approximate size (in.): 39 x 24 x 26
Materials: ebony, figured holly, maple burl, pink ivory, deerskin

DINING TABLE
Approximate size (in.): 30 x 84
Materials: various woods, bone, silver,
   pewter, lapis lazuli, steel

DETAIL

GAMING TABLE
Approximate size (in.): 31 x 26 x 26
Materials: pear, ebony, holly, cherry

43 Bradford St.
West Concord, MA 01742
(978) 371-1809
FAX (978) 371-1809
102220,1476@compuserve.com

DESIGN CHARGES:	$200 for initial sketches not rolled into purchase price; additional design fees rolled into purchase price
DEPOSIT:	70% with balance due on completion
LEAD TIME:	inquire
LOCAL DELIVERY:	free
LONG DISTANCE:	best available shipper, plus crating charge

Studio Furniture

"It may be best for buyers of custom furniture to make their first purchase a finished piece from a show so as to be completely clear about what is being purchased."

MIGUEL GOMEZ-IBAÑEZ is careful to point out that his furniture is not reproduction work, although it clearly evokes 17th- and 18th-century originals. Instead, it is "furniture with a memory of older forms and methods of construction." In the service of this memory, Gomez-Ibañez has trained in the use of period-appropriate hand tools and shop techniques.

Although a relative newcomer to the ranks of full-time furniture makers, Gomez-Ibañez brings to his craft the experience he gained in his previous career as an architect, experience that impacts his approach to woodworking in two ways. First, he recognizes that a piece of furniture, like a building, presents the designer with a problem that must be solved in terms of its intended use and its intended site. Second, the ultimate goal of any commission, in the realm of architecture or furniture, is the creation of an object in which both designer and client can take a measure of satisfaction.

His work has appeared in several exhibitions in the Boston area.

WORK TABLE
Approximate size (in.): 30 x 20 x 16
Materials: mahogany, bird's-eye
    maple, curly maple

CHEST OF DRAWERS
Approximate size (in.): 18 x 15 x 10
Materials: walnut, purpleheart, ebony

DETAIL

HIGH CHEST OF DRAWERS

Approximate size (in.): 68 x 38 x 21
Materials: cherry, madrone burl, Carpathian elm burl,
    purpleheart, bloodwood

Miguel Gomez-Ibañez
544 Wellesley St.
Weston, MA 02493-1015
(781) 710-7007
FAX (781) 237-5702
gomez-ibanez@msn.com

DESIGN CHARGES:	inquire
DEPOSIT:	inquire
LEAD TIME:	inquire
LOCAL DELIVERY:	inquire
LONG DISTANCE:	inquire

Ted Blachly Furniture

"Fine furniture making is a way of life. It is setting oneself to work in a manner where all aspects of the design and execution of a piece are done thoughtfully with close attention to detail."

TED BLACHLY prizes serenity, both as a quality in his completed work and as an atmosphere to be maintained during the execution of that work. His focus on serenity is apparent in the language he uses to describe his pieces. When he refers to the shapes he creates, he identifies them as "gently curved." When he speaks about his approach to design and execution, he describes those processes as done thoughtfully. When he talks about the finished work, he refers to it as a comfort to live with. Blachly began preparing for a career in woodworking by earning a B.A. in fine art from New England College. He spent a decade working as an antique house restoration specialist, then in 1985 he became a full-time maker of custom furniture and cabinetry. His work has been exhibited in New Hampshire, Boston, and New York. It has also appeared on the pages of *Architectural Digest, Home Furniture,* and other magazines.

HIGH TABLES
Approximate size (in.): 47 x 18 x 16 (each)
Materials: mahogany, curly maple, holly

MUSIC STAND
Approximate size (in.): 52 x 23 x 22
Materials: curly cherry, ash

BATWING CABINET
Approximate size (in.): 22 x 55 x 7
Materials: curly cherry, rosewood

NANCY'S CHAIR
Approximate size (in.): 35 x 19 x 20
Materials: mahogany, curly maple, upholstery

P. O. Box 216
Warner, NH 03278
(603) 456-2385
t_blachly@conknet.com
www.furnituremasters.org

DESIGN CHARGES:	approximately 20% rolled into purchase price
DEPOSIT:	33%, 33% midway through construction, with balance due on completion
LEAD TIME:	6 months
LOCAL DELIVERY:	inquire
LONG DISTANCE:	inquire

Thomas Stangeland, Artist/Craftsman

"Rarely do we make things quite the same way, and half of our work is tailored to the particular needs of our clients."

A COMMISSION for a single chair (the Blacker House chair shown on the facing page) led Thomas Stangeland into the world of Arts and Crafts furniture, and he has explored it ever since. Stangeland explains, "That project led us to a deeper understanding of the design language of Greene and Greene, which we have interpreted and expanded in a series of original works."

Although he has worked with many species of wood, Stangeland prefers mahogany and ebony, assembling his pieces using traditional joinery. He applies a catalyzed lacquer to the finished work because of its durability.

Stangeland's work has earned him national recognition. He's written articles for *Fine Woodworking* and *Home Furniture*, and his work has appeared in the last three in the *Design Book* series from The Taunton Press. His career has been featured in *Woodshop News* and many regional publications. He was also selected by the Walt Disney Company to build furniture for the Presidential and Vice-Presidential suites in the Greene and Greene style for its new Grand California Hotel.

KALMAN SIDEBOARD
Approximate size (in.): 37 x 76 x 19
Materials: mahogany, ebony, copper, brass

ARTS AND CRAFTS QUEEN BED
Approximate size (in.): 47 x 67 x 86
Materials: mahogany, ebony

WELLS QUEEN BED
Approximate size (in.): 48 x 68 x 86
Materials: mahogany, ebony

BLACKER ARMCHAIRS
Approximate size (in.): 37 x 24 x 22 (each)
Materials: mahogany, ebony,
    satinwood, rosewood, leather

800 Mercer St.
Seattle, WA 98109
(206) 622-2004
FAX (206) 622-6884
mahogany@aa.net
www.artistcraftsman.net

DESIGN CHARGES:	$350–$500 rolled into purchase price
DEPOSIT:	25%–50% with balance due on completion
LEAD TIME:	3–6 months
LOCAL DELIVERY:	$50 per person required
LONG DISTANCE:	freight, plus crating charge

Timothy S. Philbrick Studio

"Pleasing proportions render the whole harmonious, symmetrical, and agreeable. I feel that this is central to good furniture design."

TIMOTHY PHILBRICK begins with a set of proportions that he arrives at visually, rather than mathematically. With these proportions, he strives to create furniture that is "graceful, balanced, and sensuous." He then turns his attention to material, selecting woods that complement the overall feel of a piece and grain patterns that enhance the curve or shape of an individual part. All this is done in the context of furniture that is clearly contemporary, although it may evoke classic period work.

His work has appeared in many woodworking publications, including *Home Furniture* and *Fine Woodworking,* as well as in more general outlets such as *Town and Country* and *The New York Times.* His work has also been exhibited throughout the northeastern United States and has been included in the permanent collections of several museums.

SECRETARY
Approximate size (in.): 98 x 38 x 24
Materials: mahogany, bronze

SIDEBOARD
Approximate size (in.): 43 x 84 x 24
Materials: ebony, fossil ivory

SOFA
Approximate size (in.): 30 x 66 x 23
Materials: curly maple, upholstery

P. O. Box 555
Narragansett, RI 02882
(401) 789-4030
FAX (401) 789-4030

DESIGN CHARGES:	inquire
DEPOSIT:	33%, 33% in progress, with balance due on completion
LEAD TIME:	6–12 months
LOCAL DELIVERY:	free
LONG DISTANCE:	Fine Art Shipping Services, plus crating charge

Tomnay Industrial Design

"A small workshop is industry on a human scale. In this, I follow the work of E. F. Schumacher: 'Small is beautiful.' "

THE CREDO OF BRIAN TOMNAY'S business is straightforward: "Careful planning means careful design." In Tomnay's shop, that careful planning not only results in aesthetically pleasing work but also in a minimum of hand processes used to construct that work.

Whenever possible, Tomnay uses machine-tool methods, relying on slower hand-tool operations only when there is no other acceptable choice. This does not mean, however, that Tomnay doesn't value good hand-tool work. He is quick to point out that "good furniture cannot be successfully made without trained handwork."

Educated at the Glasgow School of Art in Scotland, Tomnay is a newcomer to the United States, arriving in early 2000 after seven years as a professional furniture maker in France. In Europe, his work appeared in many publications and was exhibited in galleries in Scotland, Germany, France, England, and Belgium.

BASIC STOOL
Approximate size (in.): 17 x 14 x 11
Material: red oak

TRIANGULATED TABLE
Approximate size (in.):
    17 x 36
Materials: purpleheart, oak,
    maple, glass

LOW CANTILEVERED TABLE
Approximate size (in.): 13 x 56 x 17
Materials: red oak, maple, glass

JAPANESE STOOLS
Approximate size (in.): 17 x 19 x 13 (each)
Materials: maple, walnut

Brian Tomnay
P. O. Box 382
Oregon House, CA 95962
(530) 692-1064

DESIGN CHARGES:	$50 per hour rolled into purchase price
DEPOSIT:	25% with balance due on completion
LEAD TIME:	½–1 month
LOCAL DELIVERY:	inquire
LONG DISTANCE:	best available shipper, plus crating charge

Trevor Corp Woodworker

"People talk to me about commissions when they are looking for a piece of art that will outlast the changing fads."

TREVOR CORP comes to furniture making with a background in other crafts—jewelry and metalwork. This history influences not only the way Corp designs furniture but also the details that appear on his furniture. For example, the two cabinet end tables shown in the center photos on the facing page feature copper door pulls he fashioned by hand.

Corp begins each design with an artist's eye by focusing on design and form. As he puts it, the engineering, or the how-to, "is answered later." This approach produces furniture in which the aesthetic component is primary; it is furniture that will outlast any fad.

Corp's work has been exhibited in shows in several New England communities. His work has also appeared on the pages of *Woodwork* magazine.

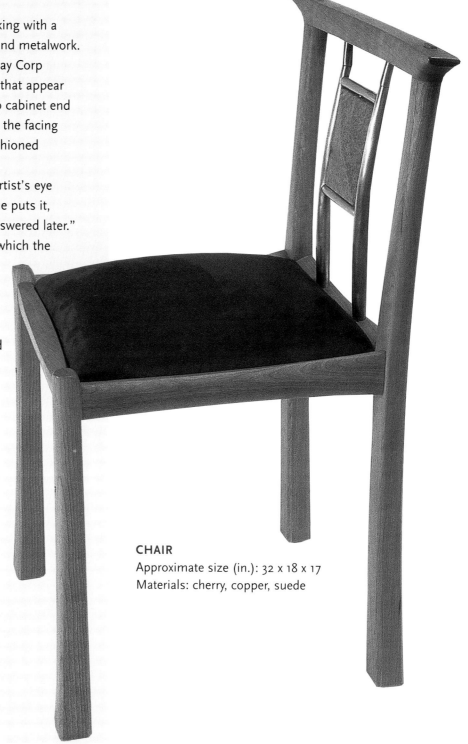

CHAIR
Approximate size (in.): 32 x 18 x 17
Materials: cherry, copper, suede

JAX TABLE
Approximate size (in.): 22 x 26 x 26
Materials: teak, jatoba, canarywood

END TABLES
Approximate size (in.): 20 x 16 x 20 (each)
Materials: cherry, lacewood,
    walnut, mahogany, copper

CHAIR
Approximate size (in.): 34 x 22 x 36
Materials: mahogany, teak, leather

2 Ames Ln.
Jefferson, ME 04348
(207) 563-6906
FAX (207) 563-2833
corp@ime.net

DESIGN CHARGES:	inquire
DEPOSIT:	inquire
LEAD TIME:	2–3 months
LOCAL DELIVERY:	inquire
LONG DISTANCE:	best available shipper, plus crating charge

Trimworks

"The inspiration for my work emanates from the relationship I have with my clients and their environment."

PAUL ZENATY strives to match his work to the personality and lifestyle of each client. This is a process that begins with Zenaty's initial visit to the home in which his work will be sited, and it continues throughout the design process as he and the client together define the characteristics of the furniture he will make. It is a process that culminates on delivery day, when, in Zenaty's words, "a space is transformed."

Zenaty prefers American hardwoods such as walnut, cherry, oak, and maple for his solid-wood constructions, although he will use exotic veneers in his larger work. As for joinery, he is a traditionalist, relying on dovetail and mortise-and-tenon construction to provide his work with strength and durability. He offers his clients a variety of finishing techniques, ranging from such modern concoctions as nitro-cellulose lacquer to more traditional choices such as French polishing.

His work has appeared in *Home Furniture* magazine as well as in local publications.

CONTEMPORARY BAR AND DISPLAY CABINET
Approximate size (in.): 106 x 65 x 32
Materials: mahogany, curly maple, glass

BOW-FRONT WRITING DESK
Approximate size (in.): 30 x 75 x 30
Material: curly maple

TABLE WITH DRAWER
Approximate size (in.): 31 x 34 x 16
Materials: olive elm, sapele mahogany,
holly, mahogany, lemonwood

ORIENTAL BOOKCASE DESK
Approximate size (in.): 92 x 85 x 16
Material: mahogany

Paul Zenaty
1736 Richmond Rd.
Hinesburg, VT 05461
(802) 482-3739
zman@together.net

DESIGN CHARGES:	$40 per hour not rolled into purchase price
DEPOSIT:	50% with balance due on completion
LEAD TIME:	1–3 months
LOCAL DELIVERY:	inquire
LONG DISTANCE:	inquire

William Turner

"I try for a personal touch, encouraging maximum input from the client at the start of the project."

WILLIAM TURNER describes his approach to design as eclectic because it includes a mix of classical and contemporary woodworking elements. The term eclectic also applies to his choice of materials. Because he believes in the conservation of exotic woods, he encourages his clients to choose domestic species as the primary material in the furniture they order. He will use exotic species for detailing such as carved pulls, edge banding, and inlay.

He is similarly open to a variety of shop techniques. For the brute work of planing, ripping, and cutting to length, Turner uses machines, but for the fussier work of joining, fitting, and final surface preparation, Turner relies on hand processes.

Turner's work has appeared in juried shows throughout the eastern United States. His work has also been featured in many publications, including *Fine Woodworking, Home Furniture,* and *Down East.*

EXPANDING WALNUT DINING TABLE
Approximate size (in.): 30 x 66 x 33
Materials: walnut, oak

DETAIL

TWIN-PEDESTAL SHERATON DINING TABLE
Approximate size (in.): 29 x 96 x 36
Materials: mahogany, fiddleback mahogany,
rosewood, satinwood

DETAIL

R. R. #1, Box 1175
Stonington, ME 04681
(207) 367-2749
FAX (207) 367-5947
williamturner@hypernet.com

DESIGN CHARGES:	$35 per hour rolled into purchase price
DEPOSIT:	33% at signing, 33% midway through construction, with balance due on completion
LEAD TIME:	6–12 months
LOCAL DELIVERY:	$35 per hour
LONG DISTANCE:	best available shipper, plus crating charge

Gregory Vasileff

"Many of today's reproductions are mass-produced and available nationwide; others, like mine, are custom made by craftsmen who are inspired by the love of the craft and are dedicated to creating the most authentic product possible."

GREGORY VASILEFF is, in the words of *Country Living* magazine, a "great pretender." He builds furniture finished to resemble antique country furniture, pieces that have served a half-dozen generations of some New England family. His finishing vocabulary is extensive, enabling him to create many surfaces such as aged and worn paint, decorative paint, scrubbed paint, and heavily patinated natural finish—all of which contribute to the effect Vasileff desires: the deception of the beholder's eye. Vasileff is proud that many who see his furniture have to be convinced that it is not, in actuality, two or three centuries old.

His work has appeared in many national magazines, including *Country Living, Design Times, Early American Homes* (which named him one of America's 200 best traditional craftsmen for four straight years), and *House Beautiful*.

TALL CASE CLOCK
Approximate size (in.):
72 x 17 x 17
Material: pine

CANDLESTAND/GAME TABLE

Approximate size (in.): 27 x 19
Materials: pine, maple

PAINTED BLANKET CHEST

Approximate size (in.): 40 x 36 x 19
Material: pine

COUNTRY SHERATON SIDE TABLE

Approximate size (in.):
29 x 18 x 18
Materials: pine, poplar

797 Pomfret Rd.
Hampton, CT 06247
(860) 455-9939
FAX (860) 455-9349
montydog@javanet.com

DESIGN CHARGES:	none
DEPOSIT:	50% with balance due on completion
LEAD TIME:	3–3½ months
LOCAL DELIVERY:	inquire
LONG DISTANCE:	best available shipper, plus crating charge

Vermont Furniture Works

"Our guiding philosophy is to create pieces of furniture that are visually and functionally appealing within the constraints of the marketplace. The cabinet-maker and the finisher sign each piece, reinforcing the notion of personal pride and craftsmanship."

THE FOCUS of the Vermont Furniture Works is period and country reproductions, a reflection of the company's New England roots and history. Specifically, the craftsmen focus on creating their work in ways that allow them to offer these reproductions at reasonable prices.

Although 60% of their work is built to serve catalog customers, the balance is done on "build-to-spec" or "build-to-fit" bases. Because of his company's small size—only six employees work in the shop—Gary Hazard feels they are better able to do this kind of custom work than other larger companies.

Cabinets are assembled from solid wood using dovetail and mortise-and-tenon joinery. Finishes are hand-applied.

HEPPLEWHITE SLANT-TOP DESK
Approximate size (in.): 40 x 35 x 20
Materials: tiger maple, brass

SPRINGFIELD DINING TABLE
Approximate size (in.): 30 x 64 x 44
   (with leaves)
Materials: cherry, maple

CUSTOM FOUR-DOOR ENTERTAINMENT CENTER

Approximate size (in.): 72 x 38 x 26
Material: cherry

DETAIL

Gary Hazard
38 Main St., The Depot Building
P. O. Box 1496
Stowe, VT 05672
(888) 822-8393
FAX (802) 253-6342
vtworks@aol.com
www.vtfurnitureworks.com

DESIGN CHARGES:	none
DEPOSIT:	40% with balance due on completion
LEAD TIME:	2–2½ months
LOCAL DELIVERY:	free
LONG DISTANCE:	blanket-wrap shipper, plus crating charge

Kerry Vesper

"My desire to make furniture evolved from my early work in wood carving and sculpture. My designs reflect a process of uncovering the form hidden within the wood."

KERRY VESPER became a furniture maker after first studying to become a sculptor. So not surprisingly, he creates each piece of his furniture by sculpting the final form from an assembly of glued-up laminations. This approach results in a body of work that is as much at home in a museum or a gallery as it is in a client's home.

The distinctive look of his work is inspired by the eroded landscape surrounding his Arizona home. "The techniques of carving, grinding, and sanding the wood to create my forms are inspired by nature's constant sculpting of the desert terrain in which I live," he says. Dramatic river beds, canyons, mountains, and rock formations all spark ideas that take form in his furniture.

His work has appeared in many publications and exhibitions and has earned him a number of commissions, including one for an Odakyu Hotel in Japan.

CHAIR
Approximate size (in.): 32 x 31 x 21
Materials: cherry, lauan

CHAIR
Approximate size (in.): 32 x 31 x 21
Materials: mahogany, lauan

CHAIRS
Approximate size (in.):
32 x 31 x 21 (each)
Materials: walnut, lauan (left),
walnut, birch (right)

3030 N. Civic Center Plaza #4
Scottsdale, AZ 85251
(480) 429-0954
FAX (480) 429-0954
kerryves@qwest.net
www.kerryvesper.com

DESIGN CHARGES:	$200–$300 rolled into purchase price
DEPOSIT:	50% with balance due on completion
LEAD TIME:	2 months
LOCAL DELIVERY:	free
LONG DISTANCE:	common carrier, professionally crated

West Bank Studios

"I produce one-of-a-kind furniture for discriminating clients and never repeat a design. My clients can be assured no one else will own a piece like theirs unless my work is copied."

RUPERT MOURÉ finds it difficult to characterize his work stylistically because he designs and builds to suit his clients. He prefers to work with those wood species favored by the makers of classical American furniture—mahogany, walnut, cherry, and maple—although, here too, the client's wishes come first. In the end, he simply tries to lead the client to a "design of elegant simplicity."

In addition to using traditional forms of joinery, Mouré is also a modernist, making use of machine-cut mortises and tenons as well as slot-fit plates. He is similarly eclectic in his approach to materials. Although he prefers solid-wood construction, he will use hardwood plywood and veneers when a particular piece calls for them.

His work has been exhibited at the University of Maryland, the Maryland Art Place in Baltimore, and the Easton Academy Art Museum. It has also been the subject of many local and regional newspaper articles.

JEWELRY CHEST
Approximate size (in.): 60 x 26 x 18
Materials: curly maple, walnut

WRITING DESK
Approximate size (in.): 58 x 30 x 16
Materials: walnut, cherry

PRESIDER'S CHAIR
Approximate size (in.): 42 x 26 x 24
Materials: walnut, cherry

Rupert Mouré
8816 Dorothy Ln.
Denton, MD 21629
(410) 479-1735
FAX (661) 761-9920
rmoure@crosslink.net
www.westbankstudios.com

DESIGN CHARGES:	$75 per hour rolled into purchase price
DEPOSIT:	50% with balance due on completion
LEAD TIME:	1½–2 months
LOCAL DELIVERY:	inquire
LONG DISTANCE:	commercial shipper, plus crating charge

White Wind Woodworking

"If I'm trying to communicate anything in my work, it is the exploration into the nature of the materials I use."

INSTEAD OF SEEING WOOD as an inert material from which anything can be made, Daniel Kagay approaches the design process by focusing on the material with which he works. He explains it this way: "I think that the 'built' environment oftentimes becomes sterile because its beginnings are in drawings and concepts rather than in the materials used to construct it." So when he designs a piece, the first considerations are the materials and how they will function in their location. He then adapts the forms and methods of joinery to those considerations.

Kagay's approach to construction relies on solid, domestic woods (as well as occasional use of veneers), traditional joinery, and hand-rubbed oil, varnish, or sprayed lacquer.

His work has been exhibited in many museums and galleries, primarily in Texas. His work has also appeared on the pages of several books and magazines.

BENCH
Approximate size (in.): 18 x 66 x 18
Materials: mahogany, limestone

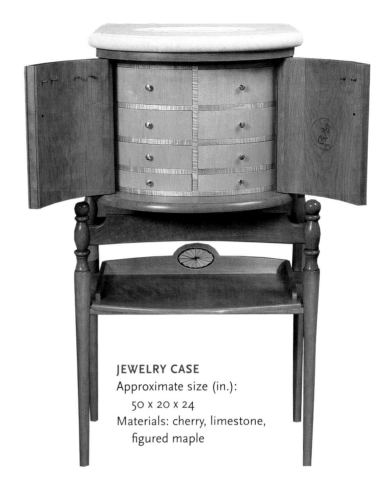

JEWELRY CASE
Approximate size (in.):
  50 x 20 x 24
Materials: cherry, limestone,
  figured maple

TABLE
Approximate size (in.): 16 x 48 x 20
Materials: walnut, ash, ebony

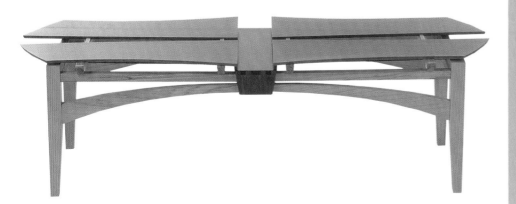

Daniel Kagay
777 Shady Ln. #1
Austin, TX 78702
(512) 389-0099
FAX (512) 389-0099
dan@danielkagay.com
www.danielkagay.com

DESIGN CHARGES:	$250 rolled into purchase price
DEPOSIT:	50% with balance due on completion
LEAD TIME:	3 months
LOCAL DELIVERY:	inquire
LONG DISTANCE:	best available shipper, plus crating charge

Wilkinson Koa Furniture

"I really believe in high-quality veneer work and personally prefer sawn veneers. I have the good fortune of having a large collection of local timber, which gives my clients an incredible selection."

ALAN WILKINSON is a rarity. Although he builds only on commission and he focuses primarily on veneer work (sawn in-house), his business has not only survived but has flourished for more than 30 years.

Most of his clients (from Hawaii, from the mainland, or from other countries) request local woods, predominantly koa. Although Wilkinson encourages them to consider other choices, only about 10 percent are persuaded. For some furniture makers that focus on a single species might create supply problems but not so for Wilkinson, since he has 13,000 board feet of local timber in his collection.

Wilkinson's work has appeared in a number of publications including three in The Taunton Press' *Design Book* series, as well as in *Fine Woodworking* and *Woodwork* magazines. Examples of his work are held in the permanent collections of the Honolulu Academy of Arts and the Royal Family of England.

ROCKING CHAIR
Approximate size (in.): 44 x 24 x 18
Materials: wenge, curly koa

QUEEN-SIZE BED
Approximate size (in.): 44 x 84 x 64
Materials: kamani, pheasant wood, leather

DINING TABLE
Approximate size (in.): 30 x 72
Materials: koa, curly koa, blistered koa,
    rosewood, ebony, wenge

DISPLAY CABINET
Approximate size (in.): 84 x 56 x 21
Materials: koa, curly koa, rosewood

Alan Wilkinson
961276 Waihona St. #115
Pearl City, HI 96782
(808) 456-1006
FAX (808) 456-1006

DESIGN CHARGES:	$250 minimum rolled into purchase price
DEPOSIT:	50% with balance due on completion
LEAD TIME:	6–12 months
LOCAL DELIVERY:	local delivery service
LONG DISTANCE:	best available shipper, plus crating charge

Windsors by Peter H. Wallace

"I have set myself the task of striving to imitate the artistry of those original 17th- and 18th-century master chairmakers by remaining true to their non-manufactured construction techniques, including those idiosyncratic outcomes that distinguish handwork."

PETER WALLACE builds Windsor chairs using the same materials and techniques as the 17th- and 18th-century master chairmakers whose work Wallace emulates. He rives chair parts from fresh-cut logs, then turns legs, stretchers, and arm posts one at a time by hand. He steam-bends bows and combs, then hand-carves the details. He shapes seats using a gutter adze, inshave, and travisher. This approach produces chairs that can truly be called "handmade."

Wallace is a self-taught chairmaker, although he did receive some woodworking instruction when he apprenticed as a youth under his grandfather, who built wooden ships in Aberdeen, Scotland. Wallace was identified as one of the top 200 American craftspeople by *Early American Homes* magazine, and his work was selected three times for inclusion in the magazine's special annual editions. His work has also appeared in *Country Decorator Magazine*, *Woodshop News*, and a number of regional publications.

HIGH-BACK, SACK-BACK ARMCHAIR WITH KNUCKLES
Approximate size (in.): 46 x 24 x 19
Materials: poplar, hickory, maple

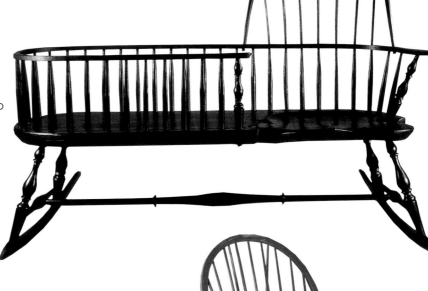

NANNY ROCKER
Approximate size (in.): 39 x 53 x 30
Material: cherry

LANCASTER-STYLE COURTING BENCH
Approximate size (in.): 47 x 44 x 26
Material: cherry

BRACE-BACK, CONTINUOUS ARMCHAIR
Approximate size (in.):
39 x 26 x 23
Materials: poplar, hickory, maple

69 Snyder Rd.
Kutztown, PA 19530
(610) 683-8224
windsors@enter.net
www.windsor-chairs.com

DESIGN CHARGES:	none
DEPOSIT:	33% with balance due on completion
LEAD TIME:	10 months
LOCAL DELIVERY:	$50
LONG DISTANCE:	UPS and common carrier, plus crating charge

The Workshop of Charles Neil

"Clients collect my furniture; they don't just buy furnishings."

CHARLES NEIL seeks immortality through the creation of furniture that will endure hundreds of years after his death. To that end, he constructs every piece that leaves his shop one at a time, using the finest available materials and traditional dovetail and mortise-and-tenon joinery.

He takes great pride in his use of rare materials. Much of his period work is made entirely or in part of figured maple, cherry, walnut, or mahogany, and his Mission-style pieces are built of quartersawn white oak. He also makes extensive use of antique lumber, which in many cases was originally sawn more than 100 years ago. The pewter cupboard shown on the facing page is one example, having been assembled from 150-year-old cherry.

Neil has been a juried member of the Virginia Artisan's Association since 1995, and his work has appeared in a number of local and regional publications.

SECRETARY ON SLANT-FRONT DESK
Approximate size (in.): 79 x 36 x 19
Materials: walnut, quilted maple

DETAIL

TIGER MAPLE HARVEST TABLE
Approximate size (in.): 30 x 66 x 25 (closed)
Material: tiger maple

PEWTER CUPBOARD
Approximate size (in.): 80 x 48 x 19
Material: cherry

Sherri Miles, contact person
221 West Lee Street
Broadway, VA 22815
(540) 896-8087
workshop@vaix.net
www.antiquesbuiltdaily.com

DESIGN CHARGES:	none
DEPOSIT:	50% with balance due on completion
LEAD TIME:	3–6 months
LOCAL DELIVERY:	$35 plus $0.75 a mile within 200-mile radius
LONG DISTANCE:	inquire

Woodworks, Inc.

"I want my work to become the fine antiques of the future, so I strive to make each piece withstand the test of time in both design and construction."

WOODE HANNAH focuses his woodworking attention on the creation of one-of-a-kind contemporary furniture. He often collaborates with his clients on the design work, believing that input from clients pushes him in directions he might not otherwise explore.

His work, done in native American hardwoods, features three-way miters as well as bent lamination. Using bent lamination, he can create the curving lines that distinguish his work without any loss of structural strength.

Hannah became a furniture builder after 15 years as a finish carpenter. Although primarily self-taught, he attended several workshops at the Anderson Ranch Arts Center in Snowmass, Colorado. In the 10 years since his entry into furniture making, his work has appeared in shows throughout Kentucky as well as at the Philadelphia Furniture and Furnishings Show.

CURIO CABINET
Approximate size (in.): 60 x 17 x 17
Materials: maple, glass

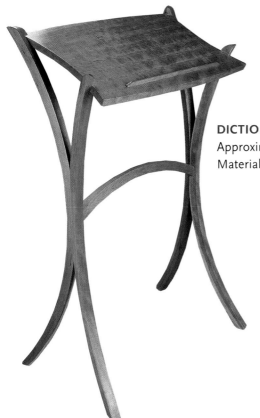

DICTIONARY STAND
Approximate size (in.): 45 x 22 x 16
Material: cherry

COFFEE TABLE
Approximate size (in.): 16 x 54 x 21
Materials: cherry, glass

COCKTAIL TABLES
Approximate sizes (in.): 16 x 16 x 16 (left),
16 x 16 x 18 (right)
Materials: cherry, walnut, copper

Woode Hannah
1760 Casselberry Rd.
Louisville, KY 40205
(502) 459-3238
FAX (502) 451-9129
wood1760@aol.com
www.kentuckymade.com-woodehannah

DESIGN CHARGES:	$50 per hour rolled into purchase price
DEPOSIT:	50% with balance due on completion
LEAD TIME:	2–3 months
LOCAL DELIVERY:	free
LONG DISTANCE:	UPS or common carrier, plus crating charges

Style Index

Regional Index

Photo Credits

half title page: (top) © Deborah Jeon; (right) © Eric Griswold; (bottom) © Geoff Carr.
title page spread: (left) © Mark Usciak; (right) © Deborah Jeon.
p. vi: (top) © Margot Geist; (bottom left) © Thomas Throop; (bottom right) © Chris Martin.
p. vii: (top left) © James Hart; (top right) © Becky Staynor; (bottom left) © Lee Fatheree; (bottom right) © Lance Patterson.
p. viii: (top left) © Gregory Vasileff; (top center) © Larry McSpadden; (top right) © Larry Fagan; (bottom left) © Dean Powell; (bottom right) © Glen Cormier.
p. 1: (top left) © Tim Murphy, Photo Imagery; (top right) © Craig Carlson; (bottom left) © Dennis Paul Peterson; (bottom right) © Neil Isgett.
p. 2: © Pam Cornell.
p. 4: © Mark Bryant.
p. 5: (left) © Jamie Cope; (bottom) © Randy Weersing.
p. 6: (top) © Stuart Block; (bottom) © Bob Skinner.
p. 7: (left) © James Beards Photography; (top) © Robert Francis.
p. 8: (left) © Gregory Vasileff; (right) © Clements/ Howcraft.
p. 9: © Michael Galatis.
pp. 10–11: © Neil Isgett.
pp. 12–13: © Ronald M. Ceder.
p. 14: (left) © Lee Fatheree; (right) © Tom Rider.
p. 15: (left) © Tom Rider, (right) © Lee Fatheree.
p. 16: (bottom) © Andy Rae, (top) © Phil Smith.
p. 17: © Phil Smith.
pp. 18–19: © Glen Cormier.
pp. 20–21: © Chris Martin.
pp. 22–23: © Lonnie Bird.
pp. 24–25: © Thomas Throop.
pp. 26–27: © Deborah Jeon.
pp. 28–29: © Jackson Smith.
p. 30: (top) © Lance Patterson; (bottom) © Ross Hickson.
p. 31: (top) © Jack Williams; (bottom) © Ross Hickson.
pp. 32–33: © James Bowie.
pp. 34–35: © Curtis Fukuda.
pp. 36–37: © Glenn Moody.
p. 38: © Tom Pardue.
p. 39: (top, bottom) © Peter Montanti; (right) © Tom Pardue.
p. 40: © Charles Durfee.
p. 41: (top) © Dennis Griggs; (bottom) © Charles Durfee.
p. 42: © Dennis and Diane Griggs.
p. 43: (top) © Kip Brundage; (right, center, bottom) © Dennis and Diane Griggs.
p. 44: © Doug Berry.
p. 45: (left) © James Beard Photograph; (top right) © Doug Berry; (center) © Kyle Bajakian.
pp. 46–47: © Lance Patterson.
pp. 48–49: © Tim Benko.
p. 50: © Robert Hodgetts.
p. 51: (top, right) © Robert Hodgetts; (bottom) © Michael Lichter.
p. 52: © Tom Nesbitt.
p. 53: (top, right) © Dean Jackson; (bottom) © Pam Carnell.
pp. 54–55: © Greg Hubbard.
pp. 56–57: © Steven De Paul.
pp. 58–59: © Cook Nelson.
pp. 60–61: © Jeff Zagun.
pp. 62–63: © Dean Powell.
pp. 64–65: © Jamie Cope.
pp. 66–67: © Lee Thomas.

pp. 68–69: © Gant Hughes.
pp. 70–71: © Seth Janofsky.
pp. 72–73: © Charley Freilberg.
pp. 74–75: © Lance Patterson.
pp. 76–77: © Rob Ratkowski.
pp. 78–79: © Dean Powell.
pp. 80–81: © Bill Truslow.
pp. 82–83: © Todd Bush.
pp. 84–85: © Elijah Cobb.
pp. 86–87: © Ken D'Ambrosio.
pp. 88–89: © Jeffrey P. Greene.
p. 90: © Stretch Tuemler.
p. 91: (top, center) © Dennis Griggs, (bottom) © Stretch Tuemler.
p. 92: © Paul Nurnberg.
p. 93: (top) © Paul Nurmberg; (bottom) © Tim Rhoad.
pp. 94–95: © SchoppleinStudio.com.
pp. 96–97: © Rob S. Wilke (RobWilke.com).
pp. 98–99: © Roger Heitzman.
pp. 100–101: © Curtis Almquist.
pp. 102–103: © Ian Ingersoll.
pp. 104–105: © Kendl Monn.
p. 106: © Joseph Gruber.
p. 107: (top) © Jerry Manis; (center) © Joseph Gruber; (bottom) © Jerry Mannis.
p. 108: © Dean Powell.
p. 109: (top) © Robertson and de Rham; (bottom) © Dean Powell.
pp. 110–111: © Seth Janofsky.
p. 112: © Dan Gair.
p. 113: (top) © Dan Gair; (center, bottom) © Paul Mangion.
p. 114: (bottom) © Steve Viale; (top) © Eric Griswold.
p. 115: © Eric Griswold.
p. 116: (top) © Stuart Block; (bottom) © Jeff Miller.
p. 117: (top, center) © Stuart Block; (bottom) © Tanya Tucka.
p. 118: (top) © Robin Robin; (bottom) © Philip Dresser.
p. 119: © Philip Dresser.
pp. 120–121: © John Kapel.
p. 122: (left) © John Houck; (right) © Clements/ Howcraft.
p. 123: © Clements/Howcraft.
p. 124: (bottom) © Philip Ennis; (top) © Barabara Swenson.
p. 125: © Barabara Swenson.
pp. 126–127: © Don Tuttle.
pp. 128–129: © Becky Staynor.
p. 130: © Rob Ratkowski.
p. 131: (bottom) © Steve Brinkman; (top) © Rob Ratkowski.
pp. 132–133: © Bill Deering.
pp. 134–135: © Grant Kernan, A. K. Photos.
pp. 136–137: © John Conte.
pp. 138–139: © John Polak.
pp. 140–141: © Larry Perna.
pp. 142–143: © Bruce Orcutt.
pp. 144–145: © Richard Bradley.
pp. 146–147: © Dennis Griggs.
p. 148: (left) © Jeff Headley; (right) © John Westervelt.
p. 149: © Jeff Headley.
pp. 150–151: © Margot Geist.
pp. 152–153: © Peter C. L. Perkins.
p. 154: © Tim Murphy, Photo Imagery.
p. 155: (bottom) © Russell McDougal, McDougal Photo Imaging; (top) © Tim Murphy, Photo Imagery.
p. 156: © James Prinz.
p. 157: (top) © Rich Frutchy; (bottom) © Dan Rubin.

pp. 158–159: © Karen Holway.
p. 160: (bottom) © John McDonald; (top) © Don Russell.
p. 161: © John McDonald.
pp. 162–163: © James Hart.
p. 164: © Bruce Fier.
p. 165: © Miles Clay.
p. 166: © M. Seide.
p. 167: (top) © Mary Beth Hege; (bottom) © John Scarlatta.
pp. 168–169: © Mark Usciak.
pp. 170–171: © Bruce Strange.
pp. 172–173: © Mark Rea.
pp. 174–175: © Mark Bryant.
p. 176: © Andrew Peklo III.
p. 177: © Steve Willard.
pp. 178–179: © Dean Powell.
pp. 180–181: © Dennis Paul Peterson.
p. 182: © Sloan Howard.
p. 183: © Dennis Griggs.
p. 184: © Philip Lowe.
p. 185: (top) © Susan Kahn; (bottom) © Steve Adams.
p. 186: © Philip M. Dresser.
p. 187: (top) © Philip M. Dresser; (bottom) © Robin Robin.
pp. 188–189: Brian Wesel.
p. 190: © John Ruth.
p. 191: © J. Kevin Fitzsimons.
pp. 192–193: © Larry McSpadden.
pp. 194–195: © Bob Skinner.
pp. 196–197: © Robert H. Brown.
pp. 198–199: © M. Lee Fatherree.
p. 200: © Paul Schraub.
p. 201: (bottom) © Paul Schraub; (top) © Tim Alldridge.
pp. 202–203: © Don Eaton.
pp. 204–205: © John Guernsey.
pp. 206–207: © John P. Hamel.
pp. 208–209: © Larry Fagan.
pp. 210–211: © Reuben P. Wade.
p. 212: (top) © Ross S. Peterson; (bottom) © Glenn Gordon and Ross S. Peterson.
p. 213: (top) © Glenn Gordon and Ross S. Peterson; (bottom) © Ross S. Peterson.
p. 214: © Mike Walsh.
p. 215: © Stephen J. Appel.
pp. 216–217: © Robert Francis.
pp. 218–219: © Evan Cohen.
pp. 220–221: © Stephen Webster.
p. 222: © Craig Carlson.
p. 223: (top) © Kevin Halle; (bottom) © Craig Carlson.
p. 224: © Dean Powell.
p. 225: (top) © Dean Powell; (bottom) © Jeremiah E. de Rham.
p. 226: (top) © Dean Powell; (bottom) © Lance Patterson.
p. 227: © Dean Powell.
p. 228: © Dean Powell.
p. 229: (top) © Charley Freiberg; (bottom) © Dean Powell.
pp. 230–231: © Thomas Stangeland.
pp. 232–233: © Michael Galatis.
pp. 234–235: © Frederic Choisel.
pp. 236–237: © Jay York.
pp. 238–239: © Paul Zenaty.
pp. 240–241: © Rob Karosis.
pp. 242–243: © Gregory Vasileff.
pp. 244–245: © Paul Rogers.
pp. 246–247: © Jeff Noble.
pp. 248–249: © Barbara Glaeser.
pp. 250–251: © Ron Whitfield.
pp. 252–253: © Hal Lum.
pp. 254–255: © Peter Wallace.
pp. 256–257: © Bernie Boston.
pp. 258–259: © Geoff Carr.